OTT FORESMAN • ADDISON WESLEY

Mathematics

Grade 2

Reteaching Masters/ Workbook

Editorial Offices: Glenview, Illinois • Parsippany, New Jersey • New York, New York

Sales Offices: Parsippany, New Jersey • Duluth, Georgia • Glenview, Illinois
Coppell, Texas • Ontario, California • Mesa, Arizona

Overview

Reteaching Masters/Workbook provides additional teaching options for teachers to use with students who have not yet mastered key skills and concepts covered in the student edition. A pictorial model is provided when appropriate, followed by worked-out examples and a few partially worked-out exercises. These exercises match or are similar to the simpler exercises in the student edition.

ISBN 0-328-04966-2

4 5 6 7 8 9 10 V084 09 08 07 06 05 04

Name ______________________________

Joining Groups to Add

R 1-1

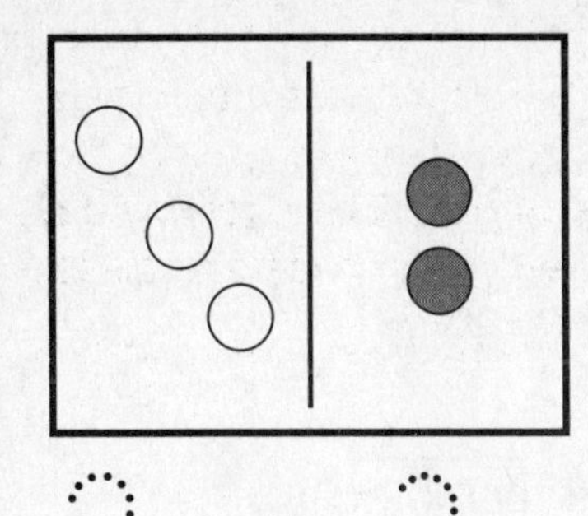

Add to join two groups and show how many in all.

3 and 2 is 5 in all.

3 white counters and 2 gray counters is 5 counters in all.

Count the counters.
Write how many in all.

1. 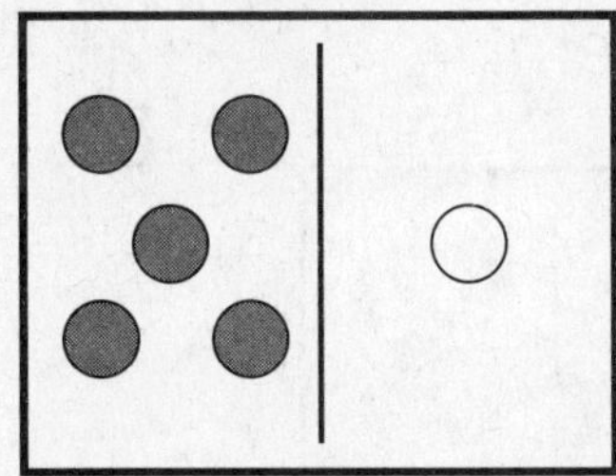

_____ and _____ is _____ in all.

2. 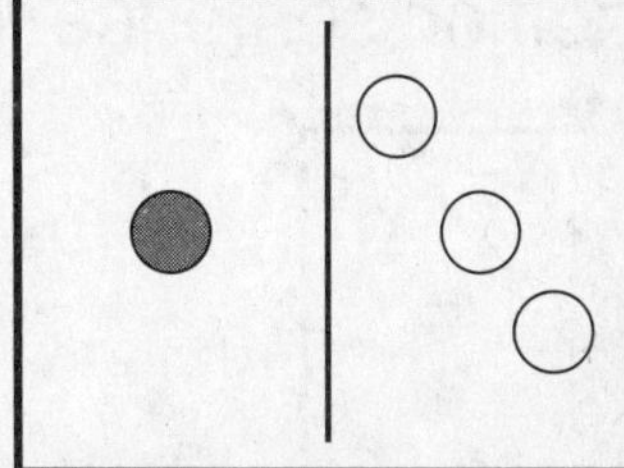

_____ and _____ is _____ in all.

3. 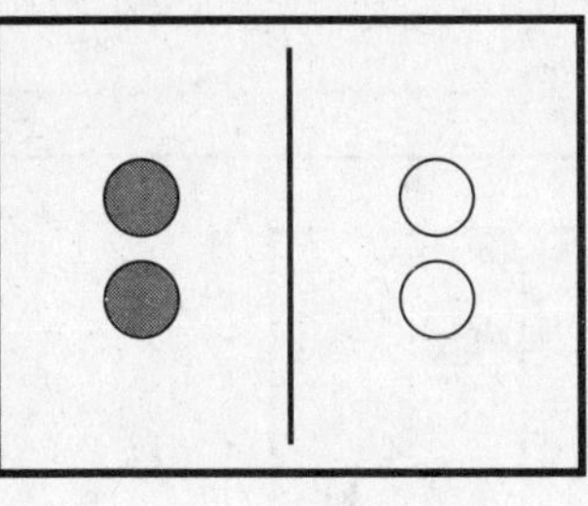

_____ and _____ is _____ in all.

4. 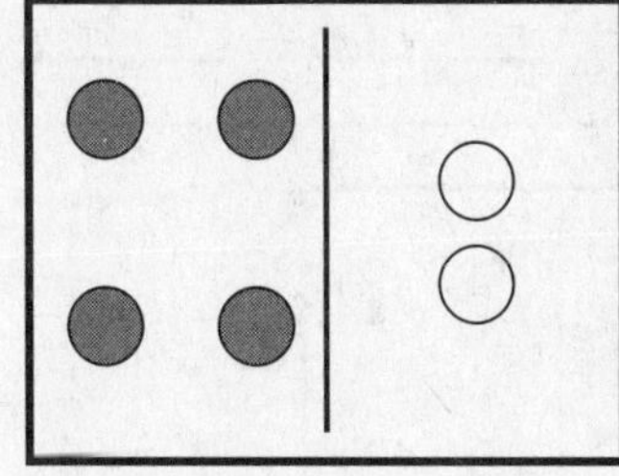

_____ and _____ is _____ in all.

Name ______________________________

Writing Addition Sentences

R 1-2

How many counters are there in all?

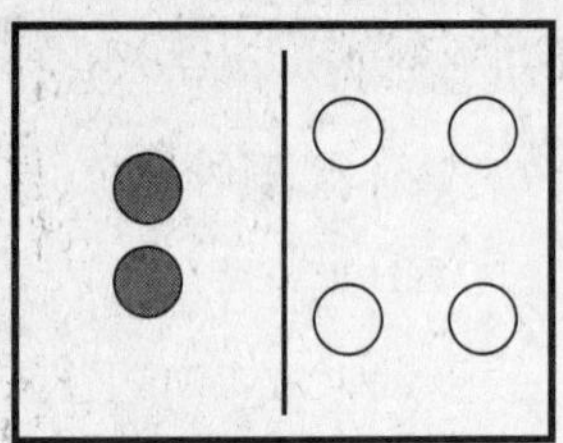

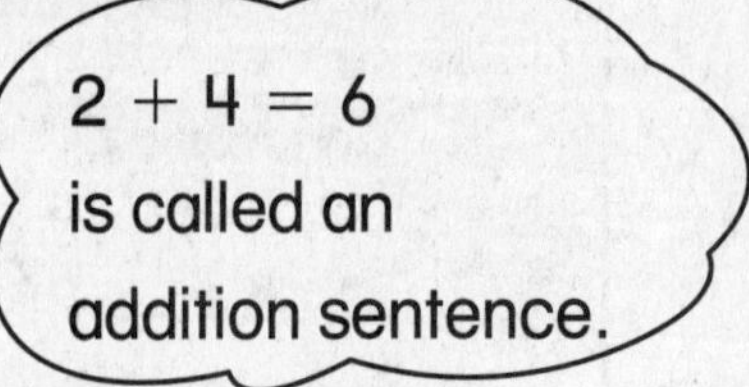

Part		Part		Whole
2	and	4	is	6.
2	plus	4	equals	6.
2	+	4	=	6

addends   sum

2 + 4 = 6

Use counters and Workmat 1.
Write the addition sentence to solve the problem.

1. 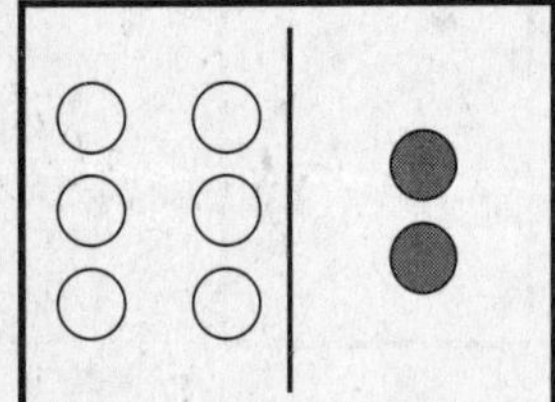

How many counters in all?

_____ + _____ = _____

2. 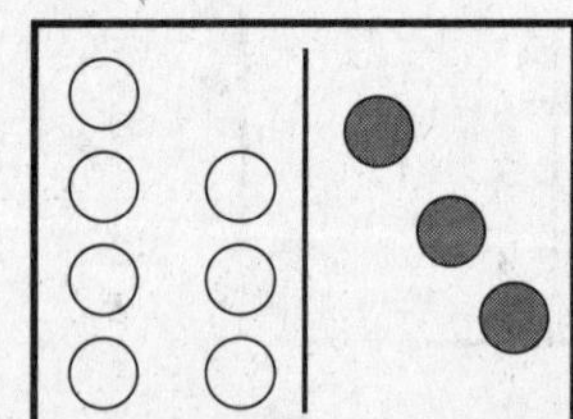

How many counters in all?

_____ + _____ = _____

3. 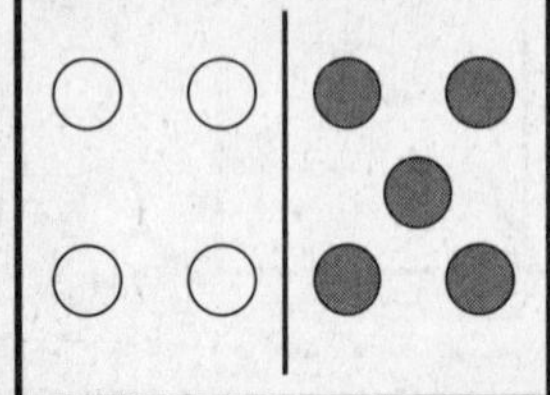

How many counters in all?

_____ + _____ = _____

4. 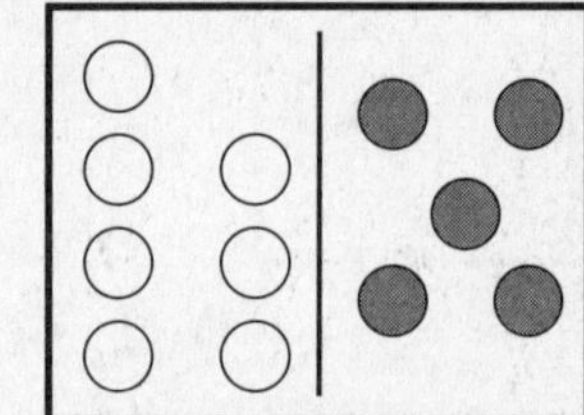

How many counters in all?

_____ + _____ = _____

Name ______________________________

PROBLEM-SOLVING STRATEGY **R 1-3**

Write a Number Sentence

Read and Understand

6 cats are on the steps.
3 more cats join them.
How many cats are there in all?

> Add to join groups.
> The addition sentence
> $6 + 3 = 9$ can be used
> to solve the problem.

Plan and Solve

You need to find out how many cats there are in all.

6 and 3 is 9.

6 plus 3 equals 9.

$6 + 3 = 9$ cats.

Look Back and Check

Did you answer the question?

Write a number sentence to solve each problem.

1. 5 puppies are playing.
3 puppies join them.
How many puppies are there altogether?

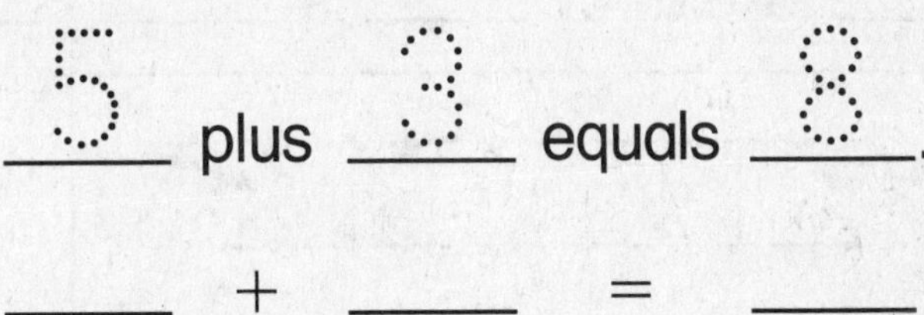

5 plus 3 equals 8.

____ + ____ = ____

There are ____ puppies altogether.

Name ______________________________

Taking Away to Subtract

R 1-4

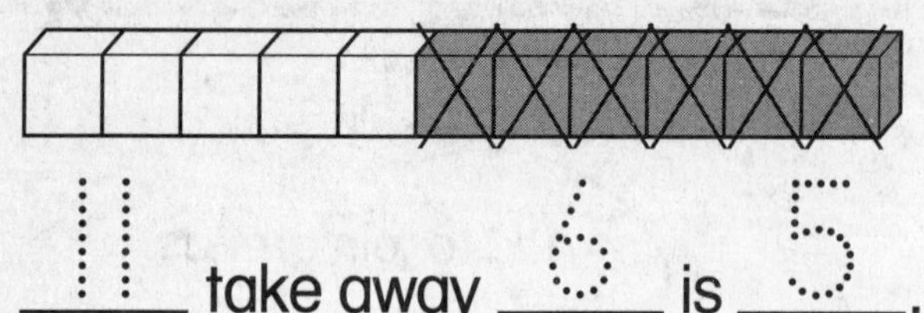

11 take away 6 is 5.

Count the cubes.
Write the numbers.

1. 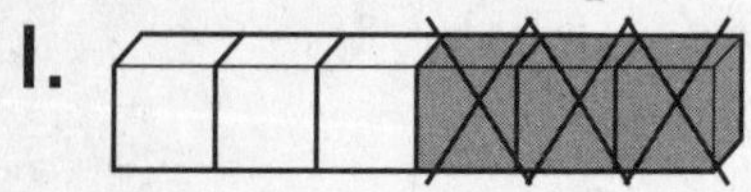

_____ take away _____ is _____.

2. _____ take away _____ is _____.

3. 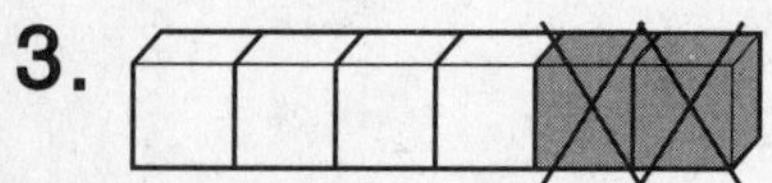

_____ take away _____ is _____.

4. _____ take away _____ is _____.

5. 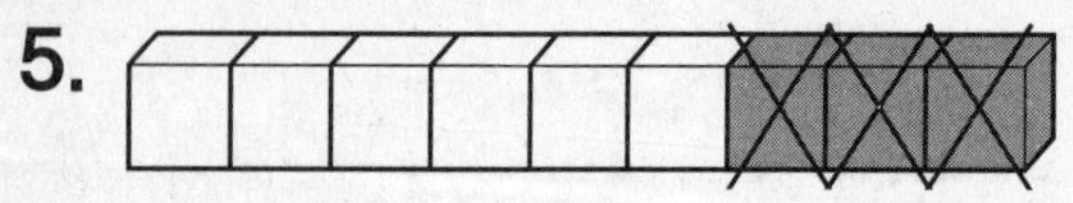

_____ take away _____ is _____.

6. _____ take away _____ is _____.

7. 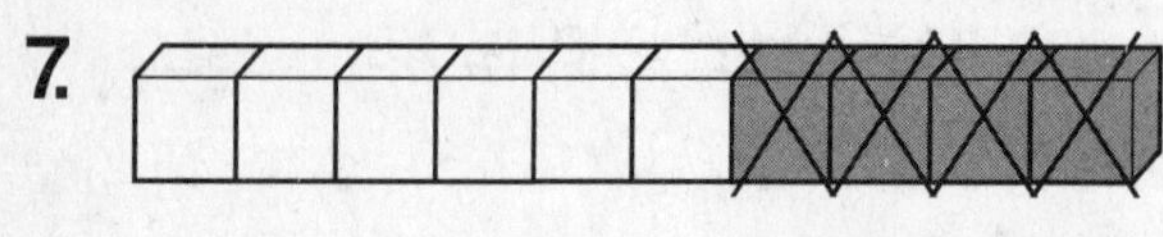

_____ take away _____ is _____.

8. _____ take away _____ is _____.

Name ___________________________

Comparing to Find How Many More

R 1-5

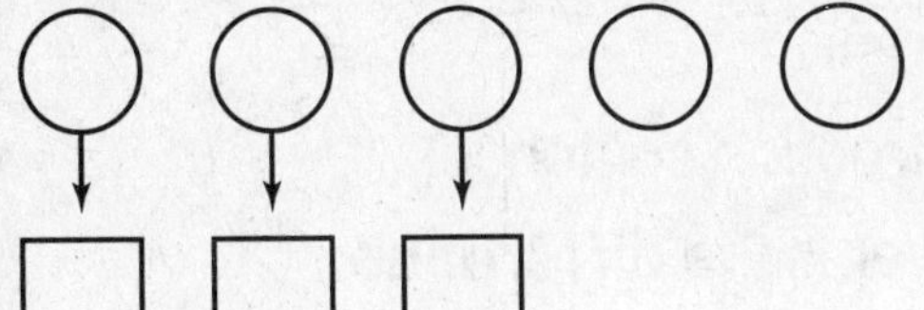

To compare the number of circles and squares, match each circle with a square. There are 2 circles left over.

There are __5__ circles.

There are __3__ squares.

There are __2__ more circles than squares.

Compare the number of circles and squares. Write the numbers.

1.

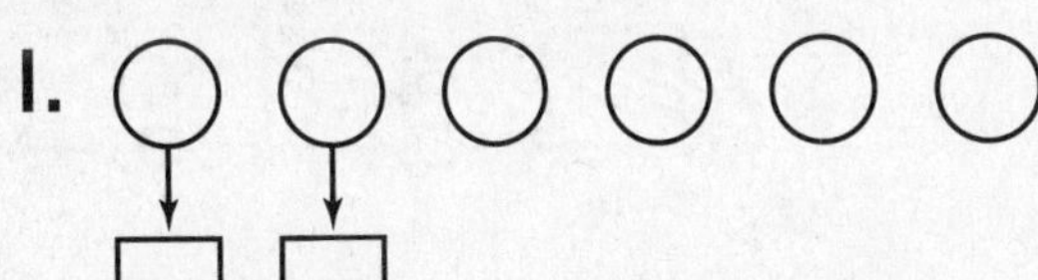

_____ circles _____ squares

_____ more circles than squares.

2.

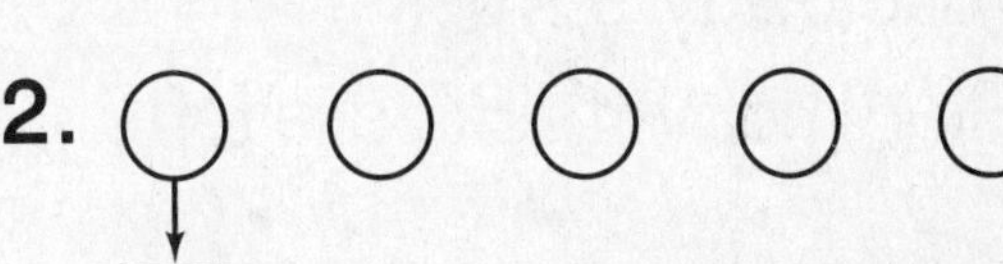

_____ circles _____ square

_____ more circles than squares.

3.

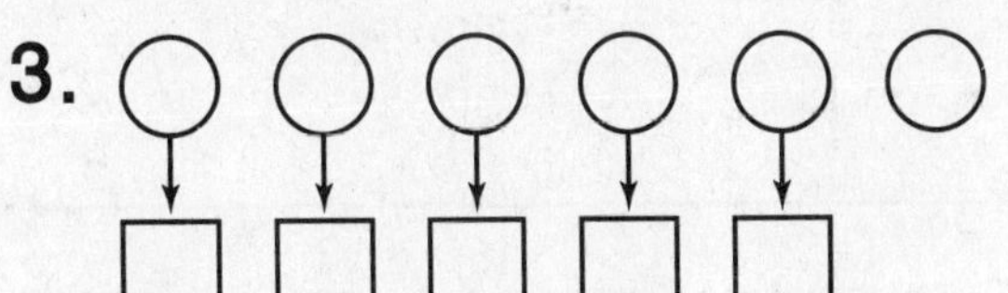

_____ circles _____ squares

_____ more circle than squares.

4.

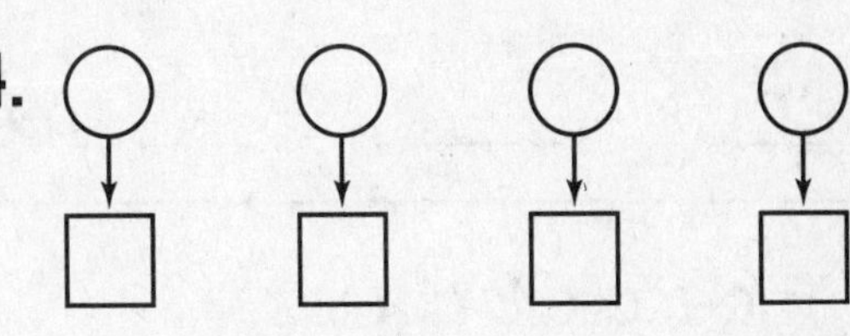

_____ circles _____ squares

_____ more circles than squares.

Name ______________________________

Writing Subtraction Sentences

R 1-6

In a subtraction sentence, the answer is the **difference.**

6 take away 4 is 2.

6 minus 4 equals 2.

6 – 4 = 2 puppies

Write the subtraction sentence to solve the problem.

1. There are 7 trucks.
   Take away 5 trucks.
   How many trucks are left?

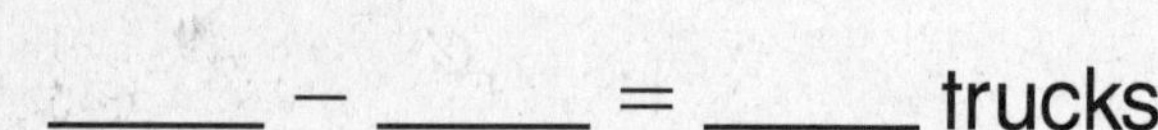

_____ – _____ = _____ trucks

2. There are 5 cats.
   Take away 2 cats.
   How many cats are left?

_____ – _____ = _____ cats

3. There are 8 apples.
   Take away 6 apples.
   How many apples are left?

_____ – _____ = _____ apples

Name ______________________________________

PROBLEM-SOLVING SKILL **R 1-7**

Choose an Operation

Which number sentence can be used to solve the problem?

5 birds are in a tree.
3 birds join them.
How many birds are there in all?

(5 + 3 = 8) 8 − 3 = 5

7 frogs are on a log.
2 frogs hop away.
How many frogs are left?

5 + 2 = 7 (7 − 2 = 5)

Circle the number sentence that solves the problem.

1. 5 parrots are in a cage.
   4 parrots fly away.
   How many parrots are left?

1 + 4 = 5 5 − 4 = 1

2. 6 kittens are in a box.
   1 kitten jumps in.
   How many kittens are there in all?

6 + 1 = 7 7 − 1 = 6

Name ______________________________

Adding in Any Order

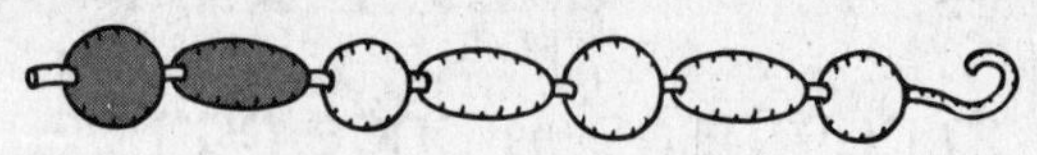

5 + 2 = 7 2 + 5 = 7

Same addends in a different order.

5 + 2 = 7 2 + 5 = 7 are **related addition facts.**

same sum

Write the numbers for each picture.

1.

3 + 4 = ____ 4 + 3 = ____

2.

6 + ____ = ____ 1 + ____ = ____

3.

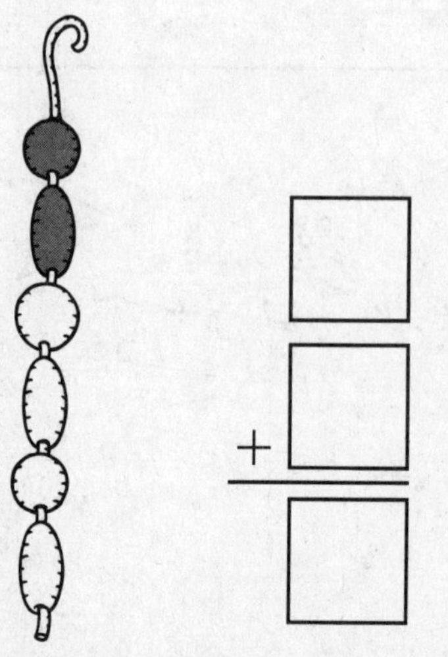

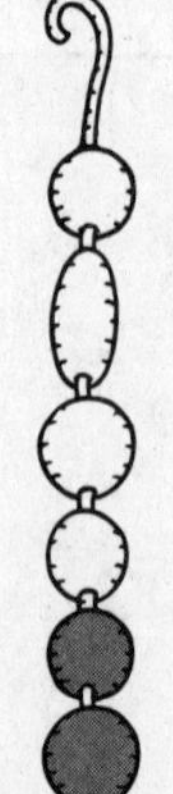

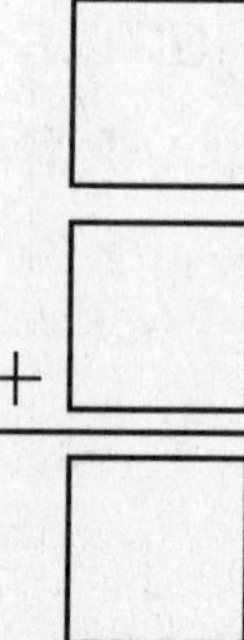

$\square + \square = \square$ $\square + \square = \square$

Name ______________________________

Ways to Make 10

R 1-9

How many ways can you make 10?
Color the remaining cubes red.
Write the number sentence.

There is __1__ gray cube.

There are __9__ red cubes.

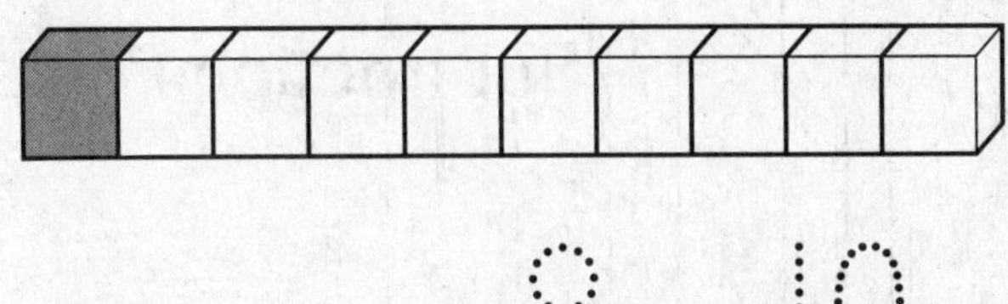

1 + __9__ = __10__

Find ways to make ten. Color the remaining cubes red.

1. 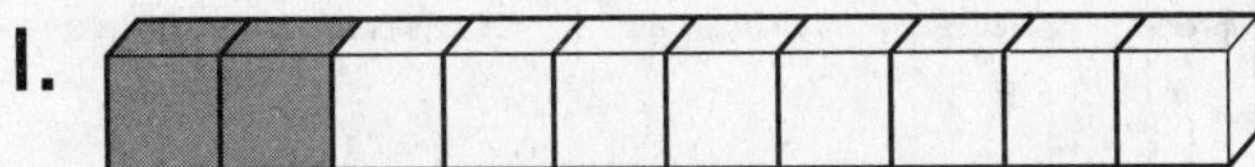

2 + _____ = _____

2. 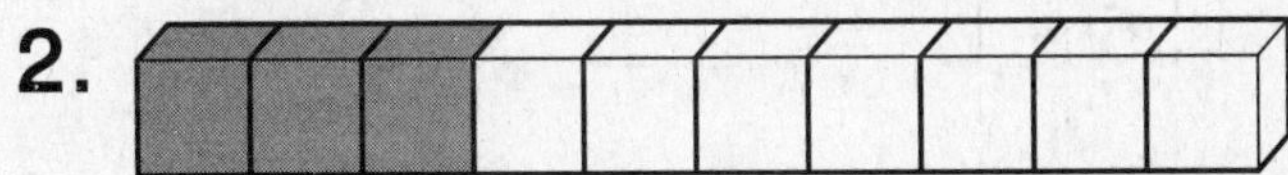

3 + _____ = _____

3. 

4 + _____ = _____

Use two different colors. Color to show a way to make ten. Write the number sentence.

4. 

_____ + _____ = _____

5. Look at the pattern.
Find the missing numbers.

10	+	0	=		+	5
9	+		=	4	+	6
8	+	2	=	3	+	
7	+		=	2	+	8
6	+		=		+	

Name ______________________________

Fact Families

R 1-10

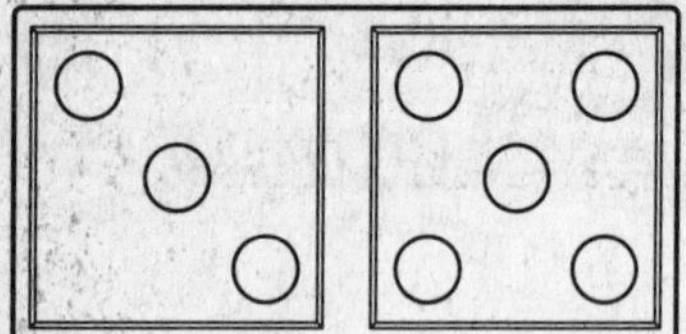

Fact families have the same three numbers.

Addition Facts

3 + 5 = 8

5 + 3 = 8

Subtraction Facts

8 − 5 = 3

8 − 3 = 5

These four related facts make up a **fact family**.

Complete each fact family.

1. 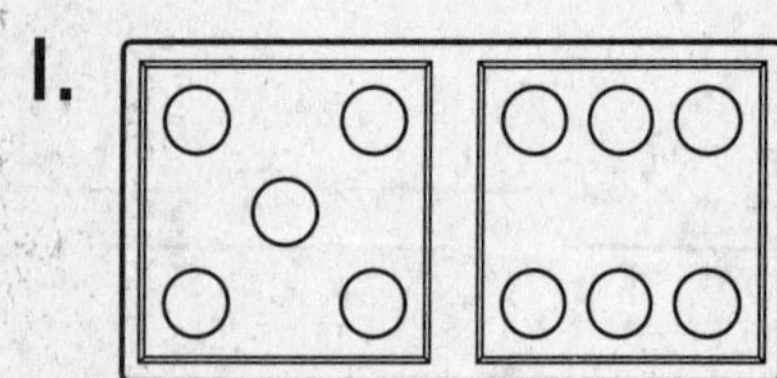

5 + 6 = ____

____ + ____ = ____

11 − 6 = ____

____ − ____ = ____

2. 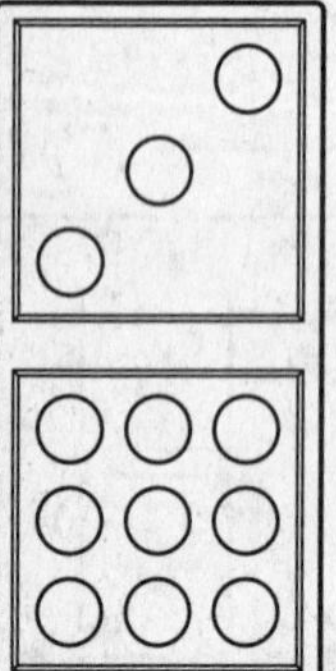

3
\+ ☐
☐

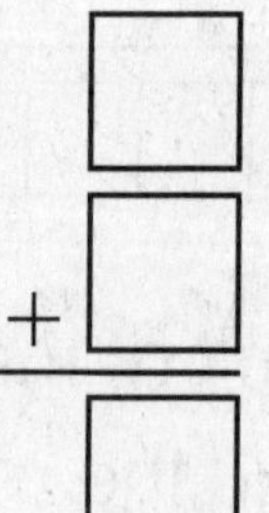

12
− ☐
☐

☐
− ☐
☐

Name ______________________________

Finding the Missing Part

R 1-11

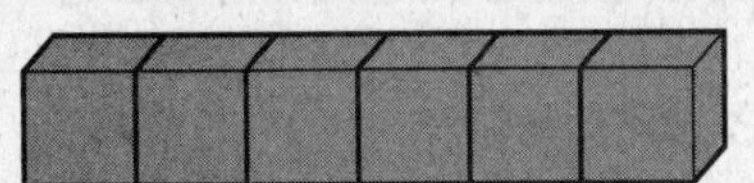

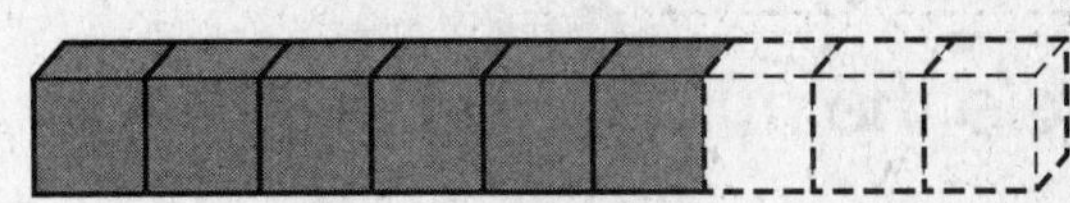

There are 9 cubes in all.

6 + 3 = 9

6 cubes are outside the cup.

How many cubes are under the cup?

_____ cubes are under the cup.

Use cubes. Find out how many objects are under the cup.

1. 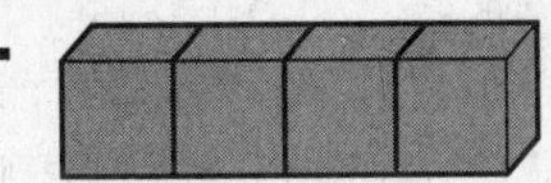

There are 8 cubes in all.

4 + _____ = 8

4 cubes are outside the cup.

How many cubes are under the cup?

_____ cubes are under the cup.

2. 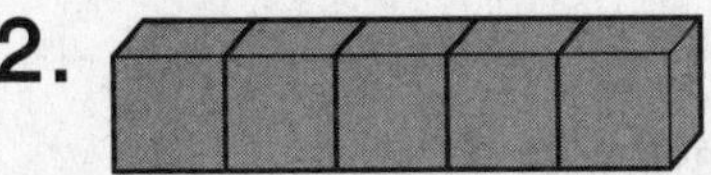

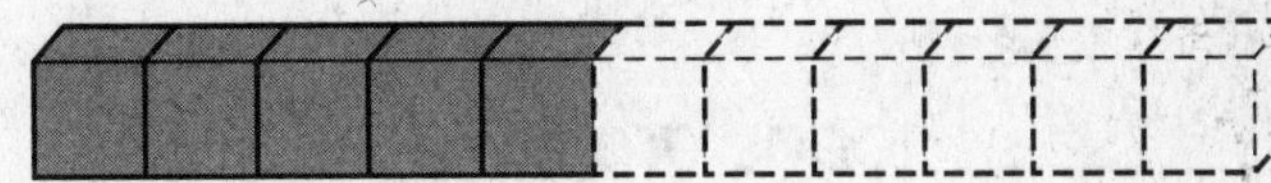

There are 11 cubes in all.

5 + _____ = 11

5 cubes are outside the cup.

How many cubes are under the cup?

_____ cubes are under the cup.

Name ______________________________

PROBLEM-SOLVING APPLICATIONS **R 1-12**

Frogs and Toads

Circle the number sentence that solves the problem.

5 frogs are on a rock.
3 frogs join them.
How many frogs in all?

Add to join groups.

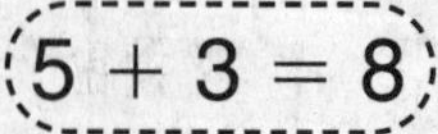

5 − 3 = 2

____ frogs in all

9 frogs are on a rock.
4 frogs jump off.
How many frogs are left?

Subtract to separate groups or to compare.

9 + 4 = 13 9 − 4 = 5

5 frogs are left.

Circle the number sentence that solves the problem.

1. 10 toads are in a pond.
   5 toads jump out.
   How many toads are left?

   10 + 5 = 15 10 − 5 = 5

   ____ toads are left.

2. 8 bugs are on a leaf.
   5 bugs join them.
   How many bugs in all?

   8 − 5 = 3 8 + 5 = 13

   ____ bugs in all

3. 6 lizards are on a log.
   2 more lizards join them.
   How many lizards in all?

   6 − 2 = 4 6 + 2 = 8

   ____ lizards in all

4. 7 birds are in a tree.
   1 bird flies away.
   How many birds are left?

   7 − 1 = 6 7 + 1 = 8

   ____ birds are left.

Name ______________________________

Counting On

You can use the number line to count on.

To add, **count on** 1, 2, or 3 from the larger number.

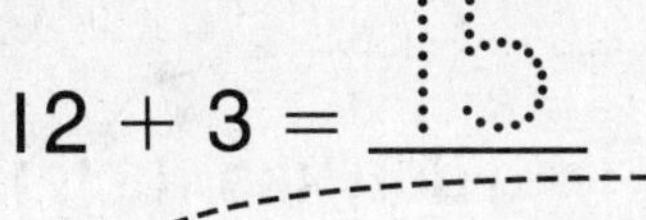

Start at 12. Count on 13, 14, 15.

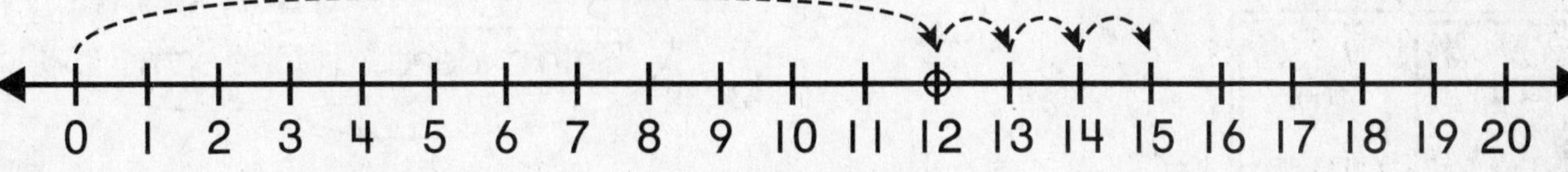

Use the number lines.
Count on to find each sum.

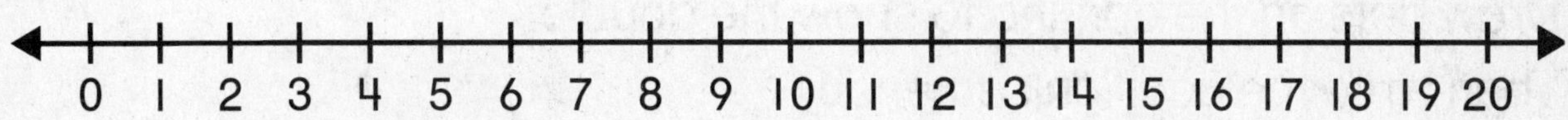

1. 17 + 2 = _____

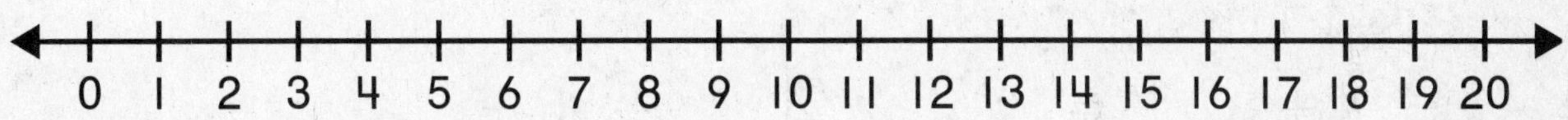

2. 14 + 3 = _____

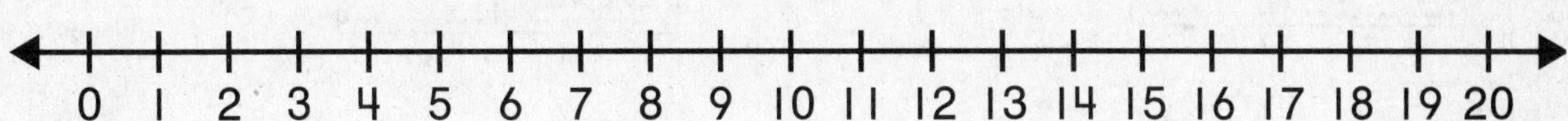

3. 15 + 3 = _____

Count on to find each sum.

4. 14 + 2 = _____ 18 + 2 = _____ 13 + 3 = _____

5. 16 + 3 = _____ 13 + 1 = _____ 19 + 1 = _____

Name ____________________

Doubles Facts to 18

R 2-2

Find 3 + 3.

Draw 3 more dots to show the double.
Then write the addition sentence.

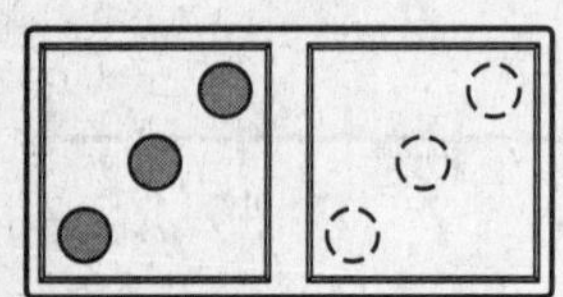

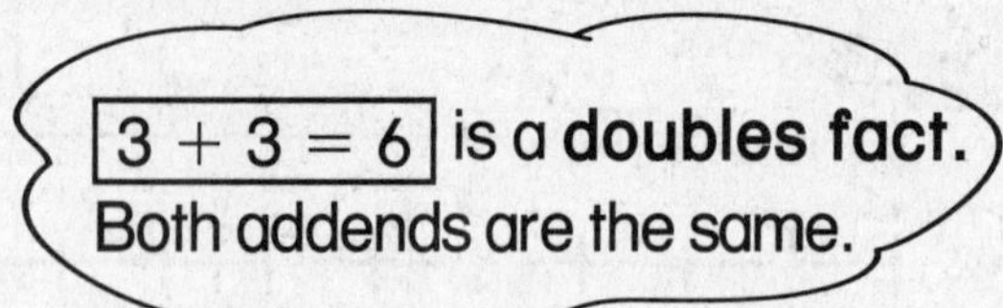

3 + 3 = 6

Draw dots on the domino to show the double.
Then write the addition sentence.

1. 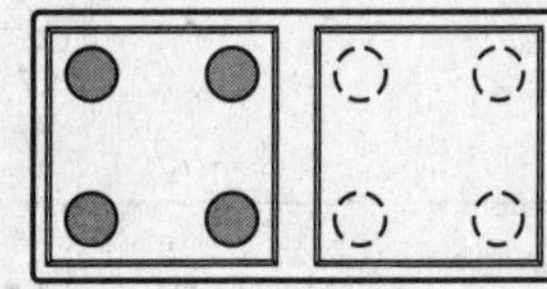

4 + 4 = 8

2. 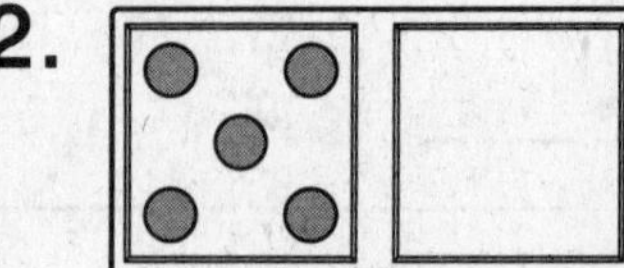

5 + ____ = ____

3. 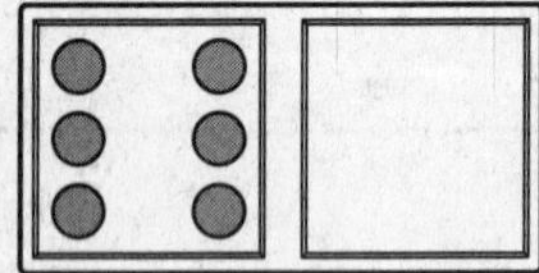

____ + ____ = ____

4. 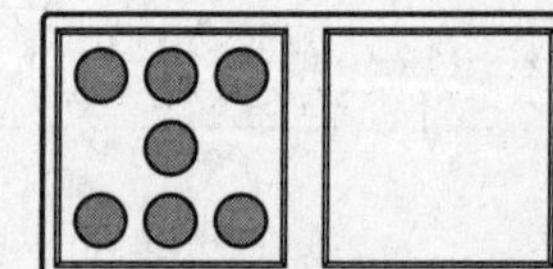

____ + ____ = ____

5. 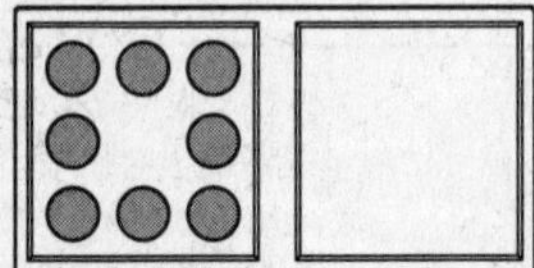

____ + ____ = ____

6. 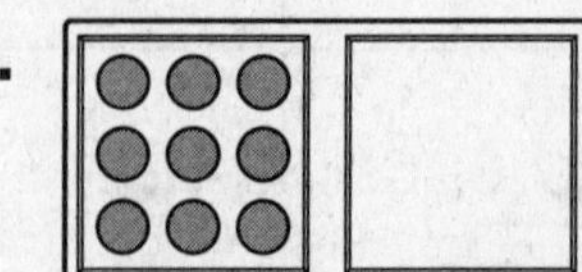

____ + ____ = ____

Name ___________________________

Doubles Plus 1

R 2-3

You can use a doubles fact to find a doubles-plus-1 fact.

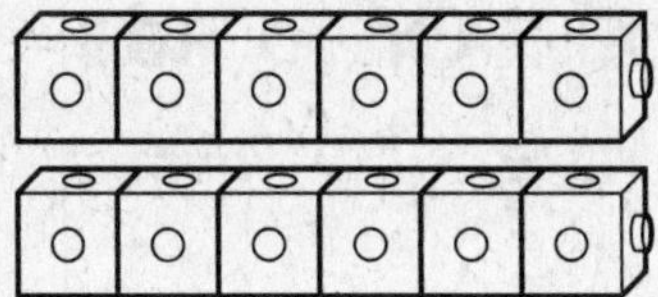

6 + 6 = 12

Doubles Fact

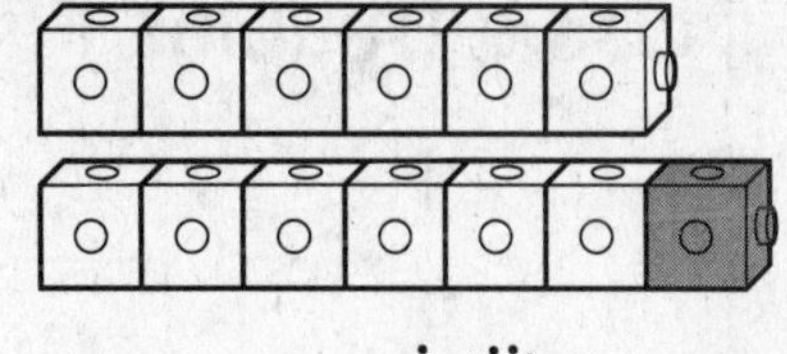

6 + 7 = 13

Doubles-Plus-1 Fact

6 + 7 = 13 is a **doubles-plus-1 fact** because it is equal to 6 + 6 = 12 plus one more.

Add. Use doubles facts to help you.

1. 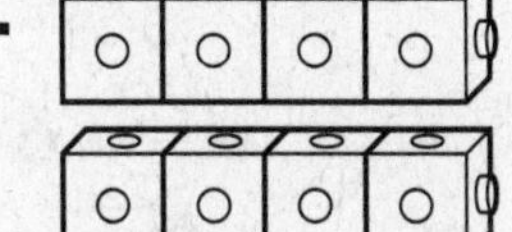

4 + 4 = 8

4 + 5 = 9

2. 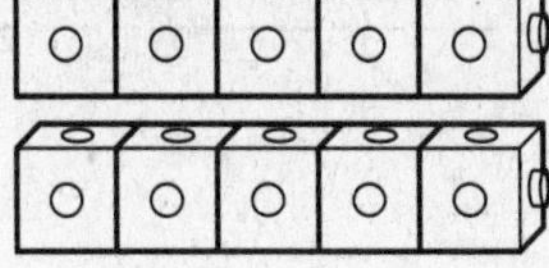

_____ + _____ = _____

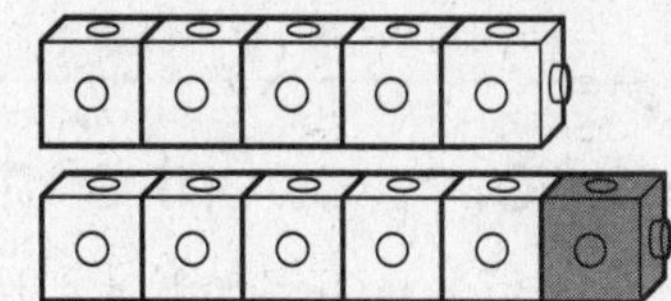

_____ + _____ = _____

3. 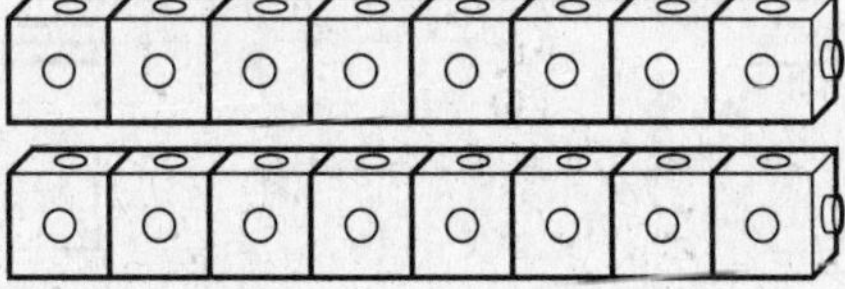

_____ + _____ = _____

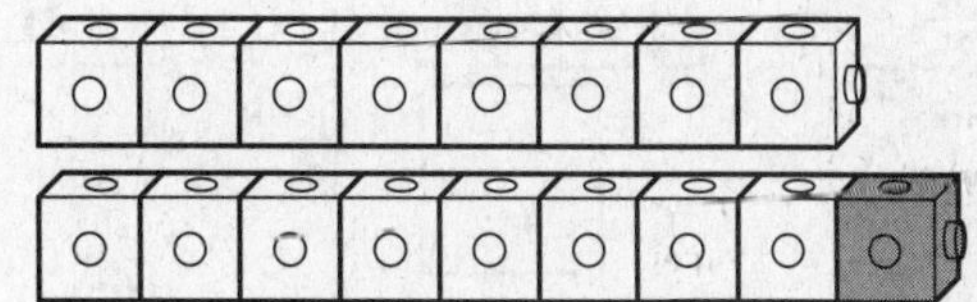

_____ + _____ = _____

Name ____________________

Using Strategies to Add Three Numbers

R 2-4

You can use different strategies to add 3 numbers.

Make Ten

4 + 6 = 10

4	
3	10
+ 6	+ 3
	13

Use a Doubles Fact

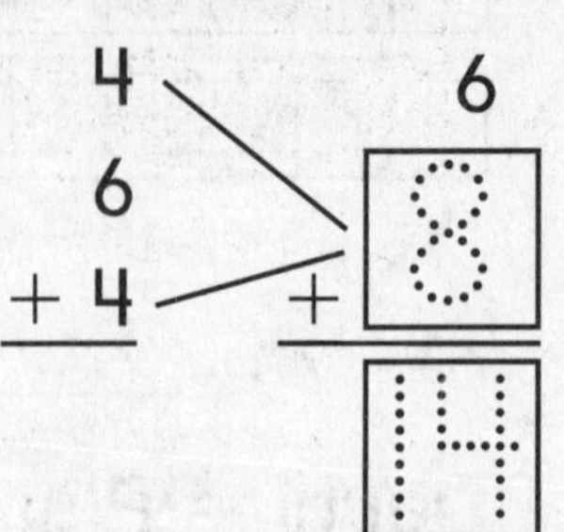

4	6
6	8
+ 4	+ 6
	14

Count On to Add

5	8
3	
+ 8	+ 8
	16

Make ten to add.
Draw lines to the numbers that make 10.

1. 7 + 4 + 3 → 4 + 10 = 14

2. 8 + 2 + 5 → 10 + 5 = 15

3. 1 + 6 + 9 → 6 + ☐ = ☐

Use a doubles fact or count on to add.
Draw lines from the numbers added first.

4. 7 + 7 + 5 → ☐ + 5 = ☐

5. 8 + 4 + 8 → 4 + ☐ = ☐

6. 2 + 6 + 7 → 2 + ☐ = ☐

7. 4 + 2 + 7 → ☐ + 7 = ☐

8. 1 + 8 + 7 → 8 + ☐ = ☐

9. 6 + 5 + 3 → ☐ + 3 = ☐

Name ______

Making 10 to Add 9

R 2-5

Find 9 + 6.

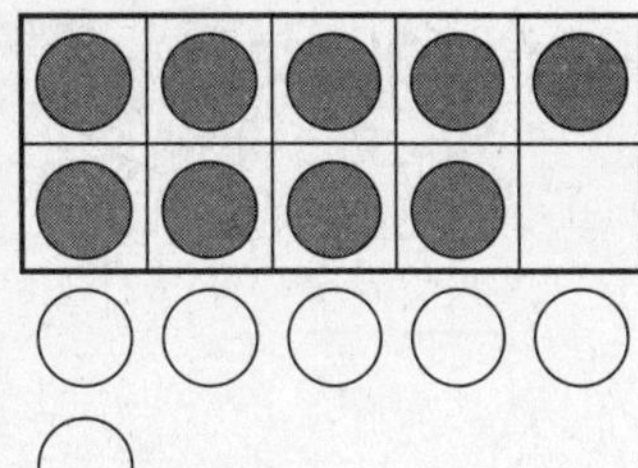

Make 10 →

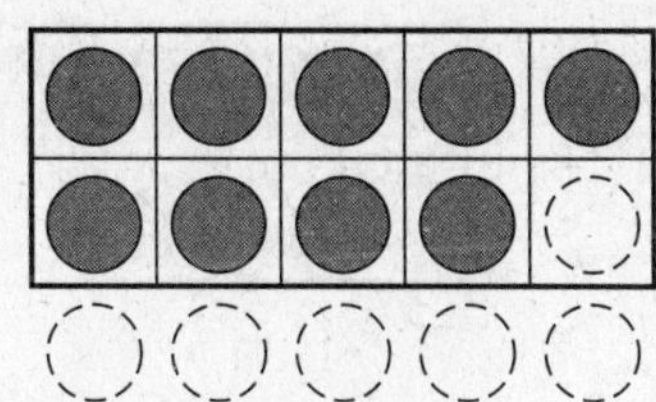

9 + 6 equals

10 + 5

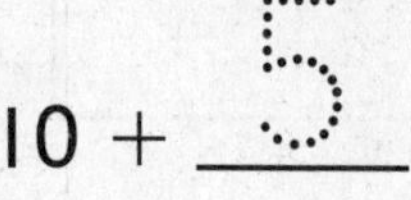

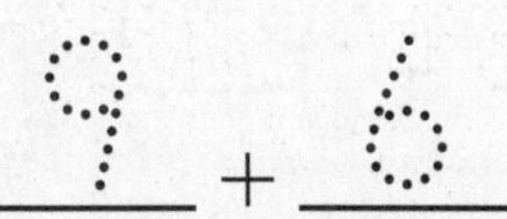

9 + 6   10 + 5   9 + 6 = 15

Use counters and Workmat 2. Make 10 to find each sum.

1. Find 9 + 7.

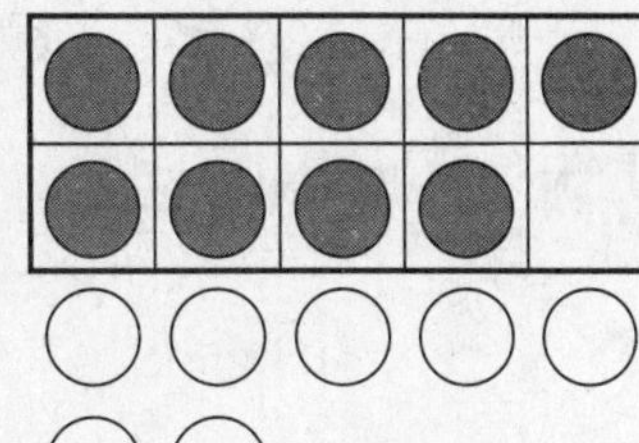

Make 10 →

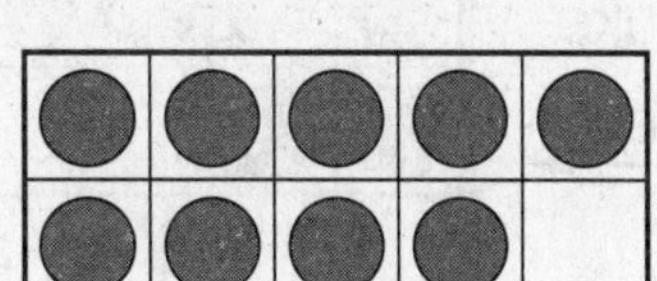

9 + 7 equals

10 + ______

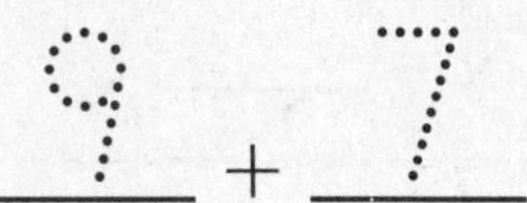

9 + 7   10 + 6   9 + 7 = ______

2. Find 9 + 5.

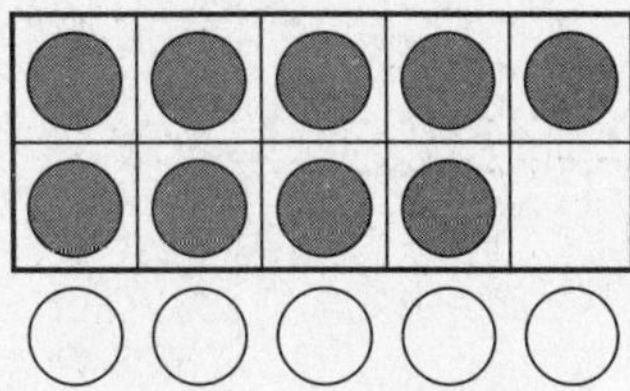

Make 10 →

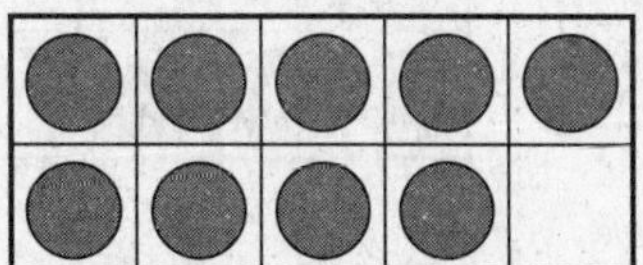

9 + 5 equals

10 + ______

______ + ______   ______ + ______   9 + 5 = ______

Name ______________________________

Making 10 to Add 7 or 8

R 2-6

Find 8 + 5.

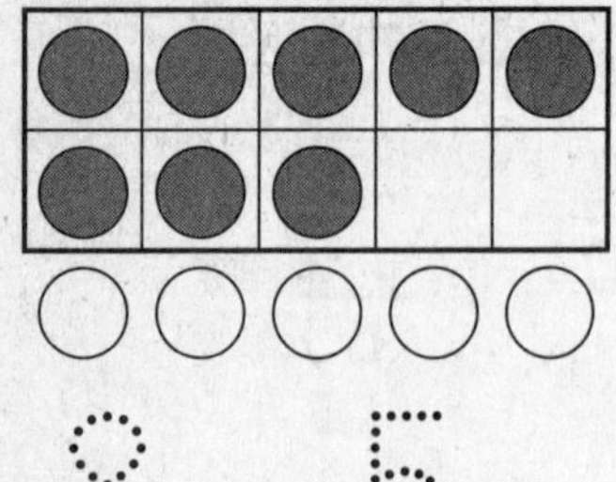

Make 10 →

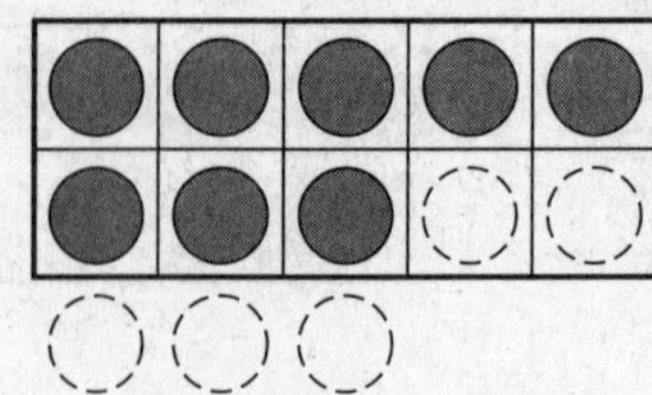

8 + 5 equals

10 + 3

8 + 5   10 + 3   8 + 5 = 13

Make 10 to find each sum. Use counters and Workmat 2.

1. Find 7 + 6.

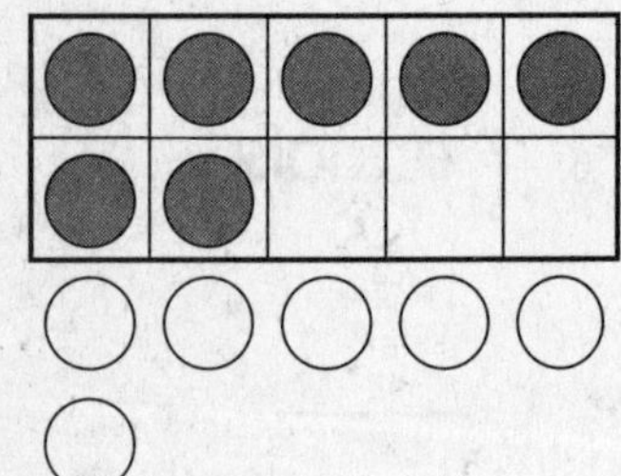

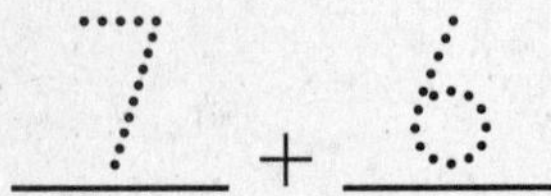

Make 10 →

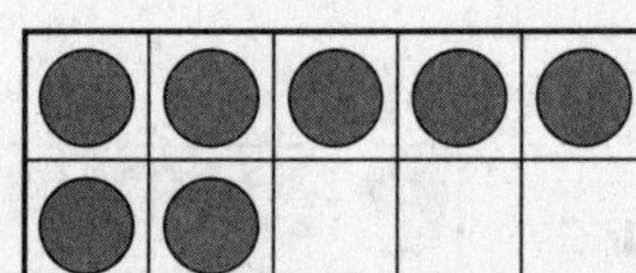

7 + 6 equals

10 + ____

7 + 6   10 + 3   7 + 6 = ____

2. Find 8 + 3.

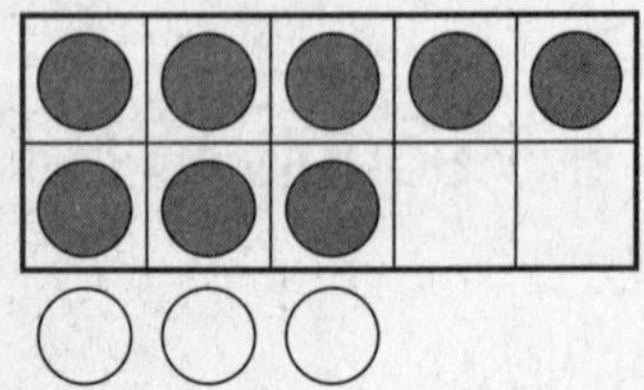

Make 10 →

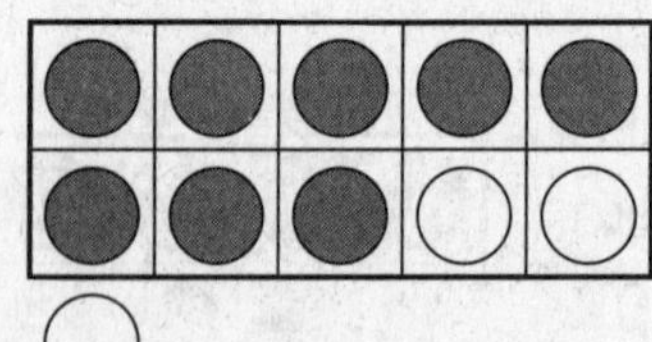

8 + 3 equals

10 + ____

____ + ____   ____ + ____   8 + 3 = ____

Name ____________________

PROBLEM-SOLVING STRATEGY R 2-7

Write a Number Sentence

Read and Understand

Tim and Rosa played 3 games of tossing a bean bag. Here are their scores.

Players	Game 1	Game 2	Game 3
Tim	4	6	3
Rosa	7	2	5

How many points did Tim and Rosa score altogether in Game 1?

Plan and Solve

You need to find out how many points Tim and Rosa scored in Game 1.

Tim's score 4 Rosa's score 7

Write a number sentence to solve.

4 + 7 = 11 points

Look Back and Check

Check your work. Does your answer make sense?

Write a number sentence to solve the problem. Use the table to help you.

1. How many points did Tim and Rosa score altogether in Game 2?

____________ = _____ points

2. How many points did Rosa score altogether in Games 2 and 3?

____________ = _____ points

Name ______________________

Counting Back

R 2-8

You can count back to subtract.

16 − 2 = 14

1	2	3	4	5	6	7	8	9	10
11	12	13	14	15	16	17	18	19	20

Find 16 on the hundreds chart.
Then count back, first to 15, then to 14.

Subtract. Use the hundreds chart to count back.

1. 14 − 2 = ____

1	2	3	4	5	6	7	8	9	10
11	12	13	14	15	16	17	18	19	20

2. 10 − 1 = ____

1	2	3	4	5	6	7	8	9	10
11	12	13	14	15	16	17	18	19	20

Subtract. Use the hundreds chart to help you.

1	2	3	4	5	6	7	8	9	10
11	12	13	14	15	16	17	18	19	20

3. 16 − 1 = ____ 13 − 1 = ____ 14 − 1 = ____

4. 10 − 2 = ____ 17 − 2 = ____ 19 − 2 = ____

5. 18 − 2 = ____ 15 − 2 = ____ 11 − 2 = ____

Name ______________________________

Thinking Doubles to Subtract

R 2-9

6 − 3 = ?

Think of a doubles fact.

3 + __3__ = 6

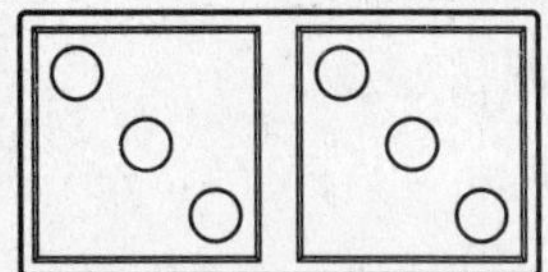

So, 6 − 3 = __3__.

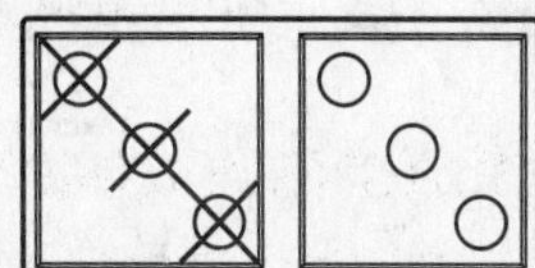

Use doubles facts to help you subtract.

Cross out the dots you take away.

1. 8 − 4 = ?

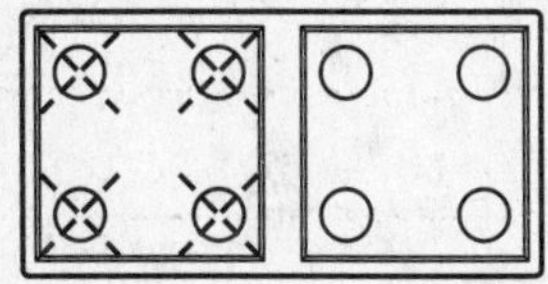

4 + __4__ = 8 8 − 4 = __4__

2. 10 − 5 = ?

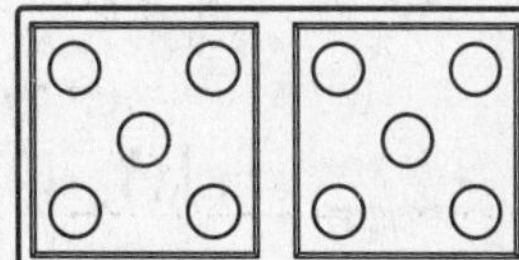

5 + _____ = 10 10 − 5 = _____

3. 12 − 6 = ?

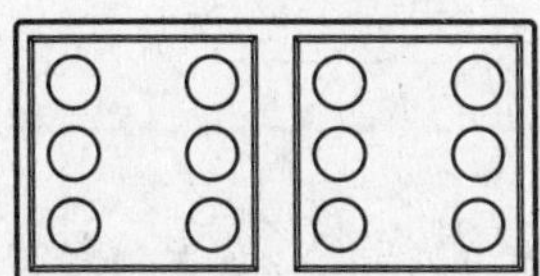

6 + _____ = 12 12 − 6 = _____

4. 14 − 7 = ?

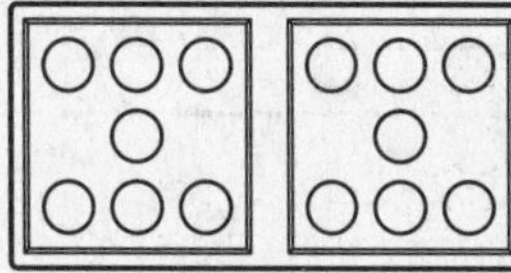

7 + _____ = 14 14 − 7 = _____

5. 16 − 8 = ?

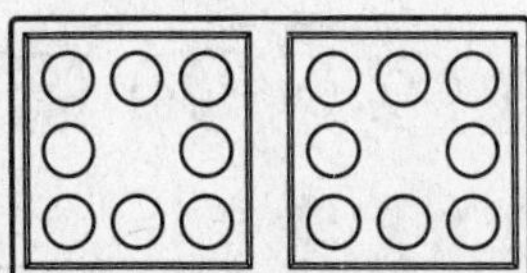

8 + _____ = 16 16 − 8 = _____

6. 18 − 9 = ?

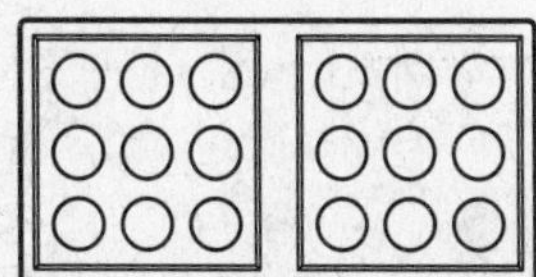

9 + _____ = 18 18 − 9 = _____

Name ______________________

Thinking Addition to Subtract

R 2-10

Think addition to find the difference for 14 − 6.

Addition Fact | **Subtraction Fact**

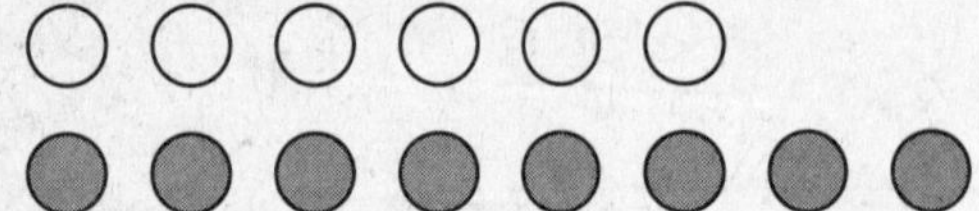

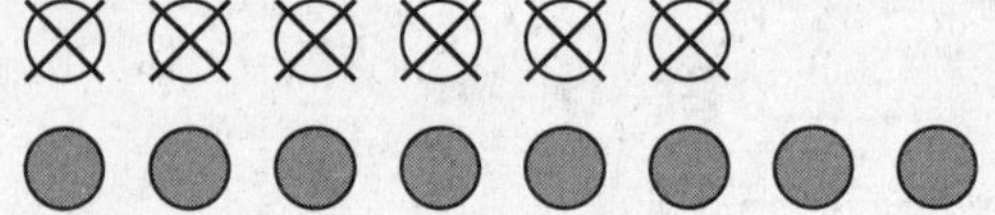

Think 6 + 8 = 14. So, 14 − 6 = 8.

Use addition facts to help you subtract.

1. Think 9 + ____ = 13. So, 13 − 9 = ____.

2. 

Think 7 + ____ = 12. So, 12 − 7 = ____.

3. Think 8 + ____ = 17. So, 17 − 8 = ____.

4. 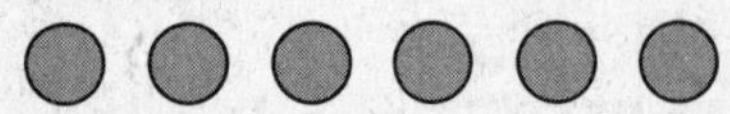

Think 9 + ____ = 15. So, 15 − 9 = ____.

Name ____________________

PROBLEM-SOLVING SKILL **R 2-11**

Use Data from a Picture

What does the cube weigh?

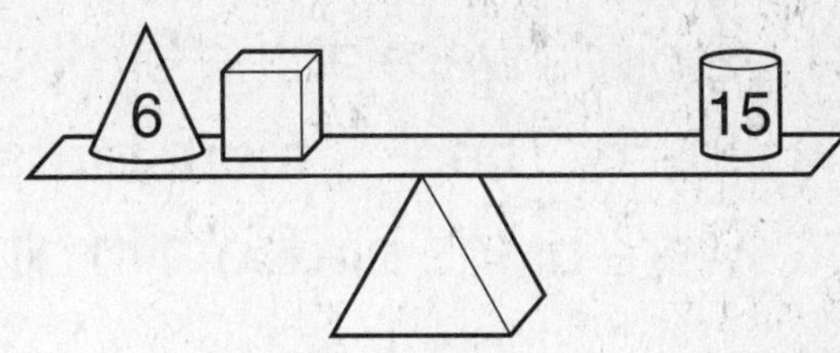

The cone weighs 6 pounds.

The cylinder weighs 15 pounds.

The cube weighs 9 pounds.

If 6 + 9 = 15,

then 15 − 6 = 9.

Use the picture to find the missing number.
Write the number sentence.

1. What does the sphere weigh?

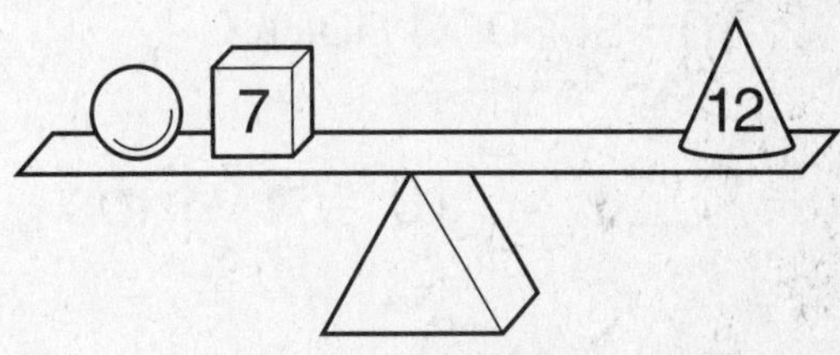

The cube weighs 7 pounds.

The cone weighs 12 pounds.

The sphere weighs ____ pounds.

If ____ + 7 = 12,

then 12 − ____ = 7.

---

2. What does the cube weigh?

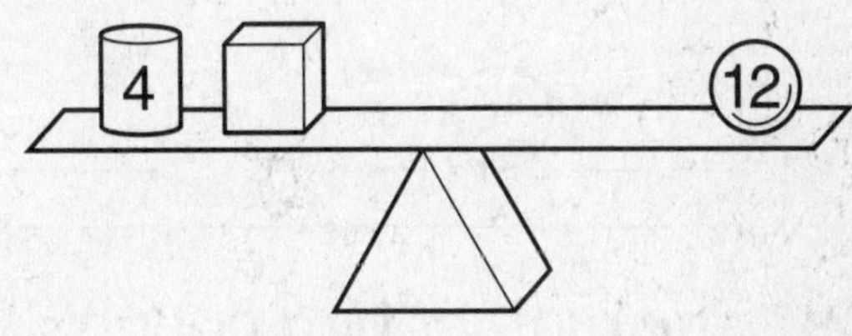

The cylinder weighs 4 pounds.

The sphere weighs 12 pounds.

The cube weighs ____ pounds.

If 4 + ____ = 12,

then 12 − 4 = ____.

Name ______________________________

PROBLEM-SOLVING APPLICATIONS **R 2-12**

Baby Birds

1. 2 birds were at the birdbath and 3 more joined them. Then, 4 more birds came. How many birds were at the birdbath in all?

   ______________ birds

2. The mother and father bird make many hunting trips each hour. How many hunting trips did the mother make during the second hour?

	Mom	Dad	Total
Hour 1	8 trips	12 trips	20 trips
Hour 2	_____ trips	10 trips	19 trips

   _____ + 10 = 19 trips

   She made _____ trips during the second hour.

3. The father bird caught 5 worms the first hour and 9 worms the second hour. How many more worms did he catch the second hour?

   _____ ○ _____ = _____ more worms

4. The mother bird caught 3 worms the first hour and 5 worms the second hour. How many worms did she catch in all?

   _____ ○ _____ = _____ worms in all

Name ____

Counting with Tens and Ones

R 3-1

A class made a snack.
The children put 10 raisins on each piece of celery.
Some raisins were left over.

The raisins on the celery show tens.

The leftover raisins show the ones.

10 10 10 5

3 tens and 5 ones is 35 in all.

Count the tens and ones.
Write the numbers.

1. 

_____ tens and _____ ones is _____ in all.

2.     

_____ tens and _____ ones is _____ in all.

3. 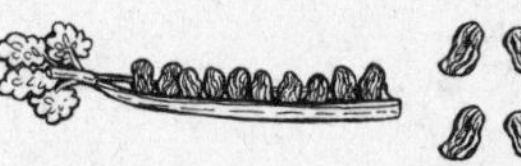 

_____ ten and _____ ones is _____ in all.

Name ______________________________

Using Tens and Ones

R 3-2

Count the cubes. Then count the tens and ones.
Write how many there are.

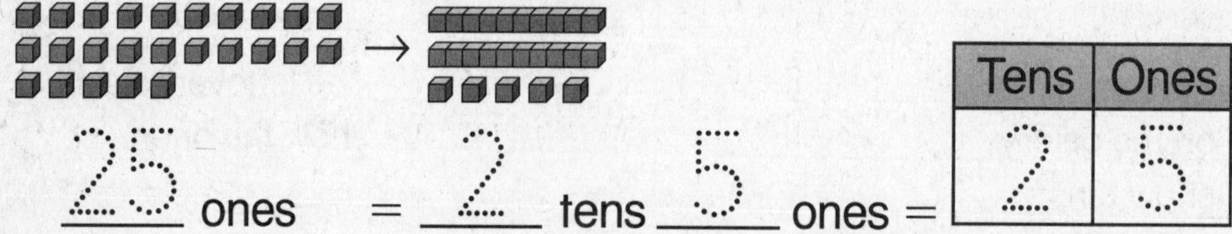

25 ones = 2 tens 5 ones =

Tens	Ones
2	5

Count the cubes.
Write the number of tens and ones.

1.

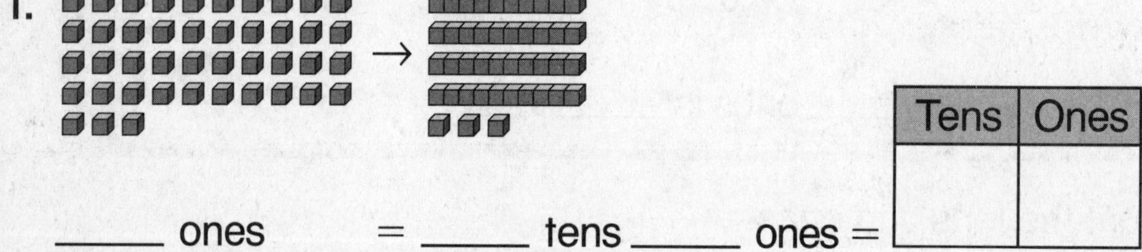

_____ ones = _____ tens _____ ones =

Tens	Ones

2.

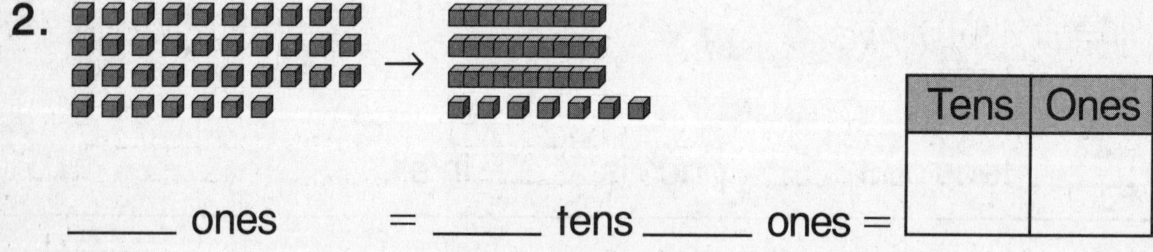

_____ ones = _____ tens _____ ones =

Tens	Ones

Problem Solving *Visual Thinking*

3. How many pairs of feet are needed to have at least 76 toes? Draw a picture to help you solve the problem.

_____ pairs of feet

Name ______________________________

Number Words

Ones	Teens	Tens
1 one	11 eleven	10 ten
2 two	12 twelve	20 twenty
3 three	13 thirteen	30 thirty
4 four	14 fourteen	40 forty
5 five	15 fifteen	50 fifty
6 six	16 sixteen	60 sixty
7 seven	17 seventeen	70 seventy
8 eight	18 eighteen	80 eighty
9 nine	19 nineteen	90 ninety

Write the number.

7 tens and 8 ones is 78.

78 has two **digits**.

Write the number word.

seventy and **eight** is

seventy-eight

Write the number and the number word.

1. 2 tens and 9 ones is ______. ______________________
2. 6 tens and 3 ones is ______. ______________________
3. 9 tens and 2 ones is ______. ______________________
4. 8 tens and 6 ones is ______. ______________________

Problem Solving *Number Sense*

What is the number?

5. It is greater than 43 and less than 52. If you add the digits, the sum is 8. Write the number word.

   ____

6. It is less than 60 and greater than 55. If you add the digits, the sum is 13. Write the number.

   ______

Name ____________________

PROBLEM-SOLVING STRATEGY **R 3-4**

Make an Organized List

Make 40 as many ways as you can by using groups of ten.

Read and Understand

You need to find groups of 10 that make 40.

Plan and Solve

Use tens models to help you find groups that make 40. Look at the tens shown in the first group. Draw the tens needed in the second group to make 40. Write the missing numbers in the list.

Look Back and Check

Check to see if each row makes 40.

	Tens	Tens	Total
1.	0 tens	4 tens	40
2.	____ ten	____ tens	40
3.	____ tens	____ tens	40
4.	____ tens	____ ten	40

Name ______________________________

Comparing Numbers

R 3-5

You can compare numbers using words or the signs >, <, or =.

Step 1	Step 2	Step 3
Compare the tens.	If the tens are the same, compare the ones.	Tens and ones can be the same.
1 ten and 3 tens 1 ten **is less than** 3 tens. 13 **is less than** 31. $13 < 31$	3 tens **is equal to** 3 tens 9 ones and 5 ones 9 ones **is greater than** 5 ones. 39 **is greater than** 35. $39 > 35$	2 tens **is equal to** 2 tens. 4 ones **is equal to** 4 ones. 24 **is equal to** 24. $24 = 24$

Write the words and circle the symbol.

1.

50 is ______________________ 52

50   <   >   =   52

2.

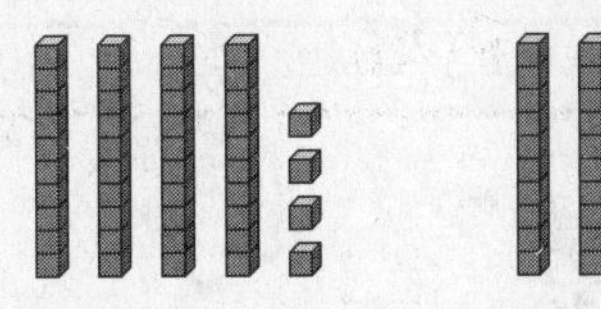

44 is ______________________ 34

44   <   >   =   34

3.

67 is ______________________ 67

67   <   >   =   67

4.

63 is ______________________ 74

63   <   >   =   74

Name ______________________________

Finding the Closest Ten

R 3-6

Are there **about** 40 or 50 pumpkins?

Use tens to tell **about** how many.
Find the closest ten.

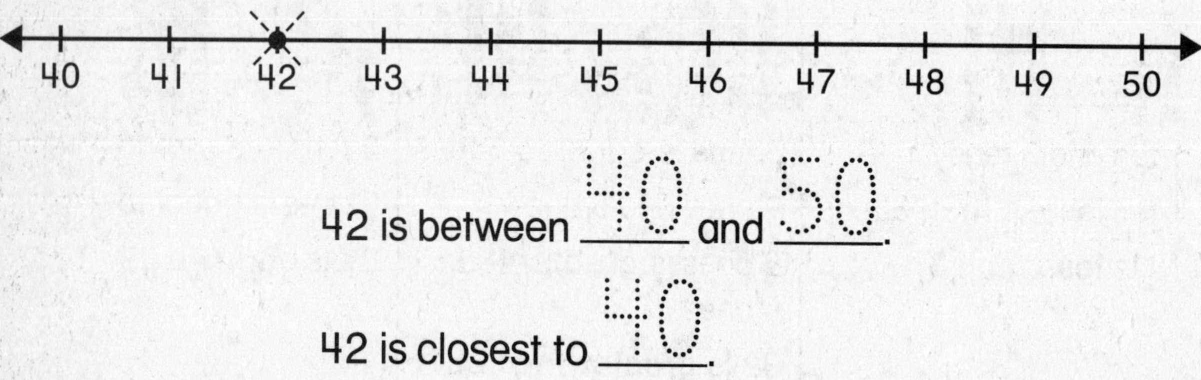

42 is between 40 and 50.

42 is closest to 40.

Find the number on the basket on the number line.
Write the closest ten.

1.

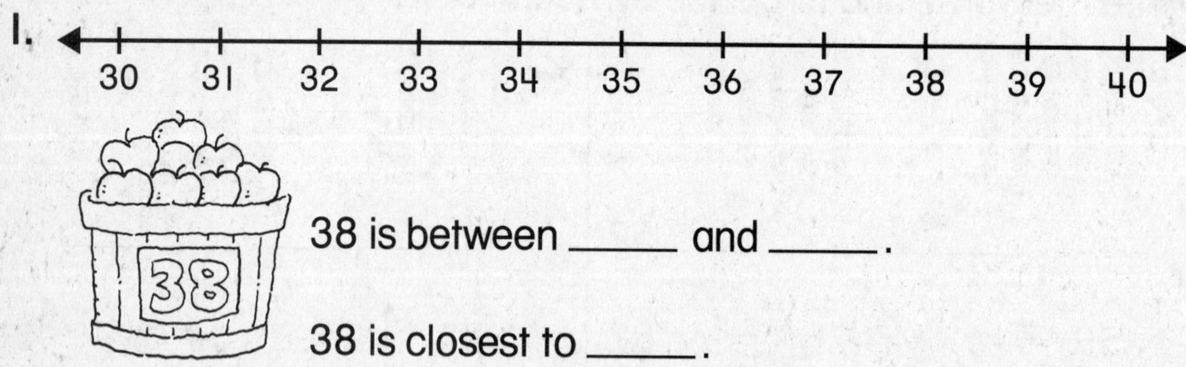

38 is between _____ and _____.

38 is closest to _____.

2.

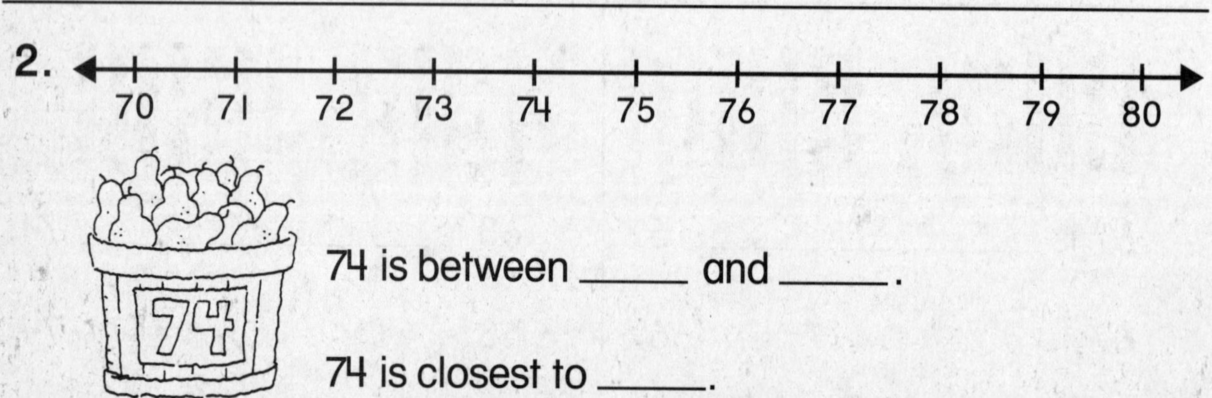

74 is between _____ and _____.

74 is closest to _____.

Name ______________________________

Before, After, and Between

1	2	3	4	5	6	7	8	9	10
11	12	13	14	15	16	17	18	19	20
21	22	23	24	25	26	27	28	29	30
31	32	33	34	35	36	37	38	39	40
41	42	43	44	45	46	47	48	49	50
51	52	53	54	55	56	57	58	59	60
61	62	63	64	65	66	67	68	69	70
71	72	73	74	75	76	77	78	79	80
81	82	83	84	85	86	87	88	89	90
91	92	93	94	95	96	97	98	99	100

Use the words **before, after,** and **between** to help you find the numbers.

One **before** 66 is 65.

One **after** 66 is 67.

66 is **between** 65 and 67.

Answer the questions.

1. One before 12 is ______.

One after 12 is ______.

The number between

______ and ______ is 12.

2. One before 70 is ______.

One after 70 is ______.

The number between

______ and ______ is 70.

3. One before 45 is ______.

One after 45 is ______.

The number between

______ and ______ is 45.

4. One before 91 is ______.

One after 91 is ______.

The number between

______ and ______ is 91.

Name ______________________________

Skip Counting on the Hundred Chart

R 3-8

1	2	3	4	5	6	7	8	9	10
11	12	13	14	15	16	17	18	19	20
21	22	23	24	25	26	27	28	29	30
31	32	33	34	35	36	37	38	39	40
41	42	43	44	45	46	47	48	49	50
51	52	53	54	55	56	57	58	59	60
61	62	63	64	65	66	67	68	69	70
71	72	73	74	75	76	77	78	79	80
81	82	83	84	85	86	87	88	89	90
91	92	93	94	95	96	97	98	99	100

A pattern is something that repeats.

A **hundred chart** makes number patterns easy to see.

Start at 10.

Skip count by 10s.

What is the ones digit in each number?

______

Use the hundred chart to answer the questions.

1. Start at 5. Skip count by 5s. Shade the numbers. What numbers do you find in the ones digit? ______ and ______

2. Start at 3. Skip count by 3s. Circle the numbers. What numbers do you find in the ones digit?

____

Problem Solving *Number Sense*

3. Count by 4s. 4, 8, 12, 16, ______, ______, ______, ______

4. Count backward by 8s.

   80, 72, 64, 56, ______, ______, ______, ______

Name ______________________________

Even and Odd Numbers

R 3-9

An **even** number of things can be matched.

An **odd** number of things cannot be matched.

Draw lines.

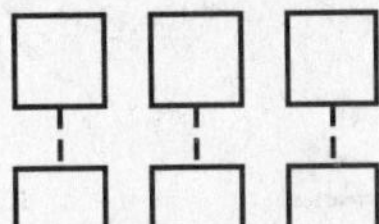

Do the cubes match?

6 is an __even__ number.

Draw lines.

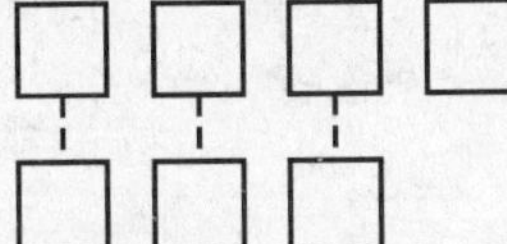

Do the cubes match?

7 is an __odd__ number.

Draw lines. Is the number even or odd?

1.

10 is an __________ number.

2.

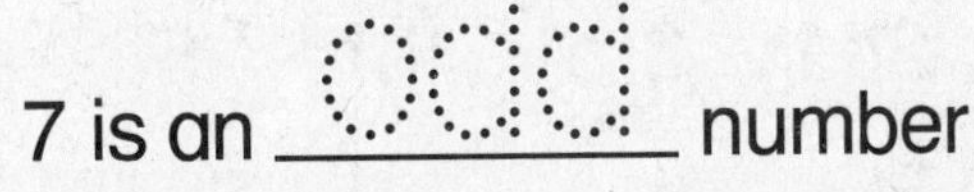

15 is an __________ number.

3.

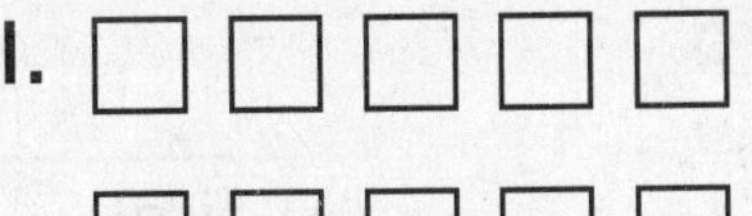

9 is an __________ number.

4.

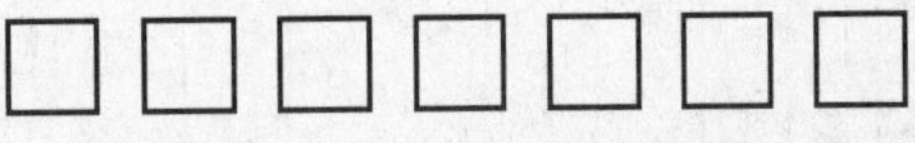

12 is an __________ number.

Write even or odd.

5. 19 __________ 23 __________ 20 __________

6. 34 __________ 14 __________ 27 __________

Name ______________________________

Ordinal Numbers Through Twentieth

R 3-10

Sometimes we need to tell the **order** of things.
We use **ordinal numbers** to tell the order.

1st	2nd	3rd	4th	5th	6th	7th	8th	9th	10th
first	second	third	fourth	fifth	sixth	seventh	eighth	ninth	tenth

Match the ordinal number with the ordinal word.

1. sixth fourth ninth first

9th 6th 4th 1st

2. seventh third tenth second

3rd 7th 2nd 10th

Write the ordinal number.

3. eleventh _____ sixteenth _____ twentieth _____

Name ____

PROBLEM-SOLVING SKILL **R 3-11**

Use Data From a Chart

Use clues to find the secret number on the chart.
Cross out numbers on the chart that do not fit each clue.

Clues:

It is greater than 25. → Cross out the numbers 25 and *less*.

It is less than 30. → Cross out the numbers 30 and *greater*.

It has a 7 in the ones place. → Cross out the numbers that don't have a 7 in the ones place. 26, 28, 29

1	2	3	4	5	6	7	8	9	20
21	22	23	24	25	26	27	28	29	30
31	32	33	34	35	36	37	38	39	40

The secret number is 27.

Use the clues to find the secret number.

31	32	33	34	35	36	37	38	39	40
41	42	43	44	45	46	47	48	49	50
51	52	53	54	55	56	57	58	59	60

It is greater than 40. → Cross out the numbers _____ and less.

It is less than 46. → Cross out the numbers _____ and greater.

It has a 5 in the ones place. → Cross out the numbers

_______________.

The secret number is _____.

Name ____________________

Dime, Nickel, and Penny

R 3-12

dime
10 cents
10¢

Count dimes by tens.

10¢ ______ 20¢ ______

nickel
5 cents
5¢

Count nickels by fives.

penny
1 cent
1¢

Count pennies by ones.

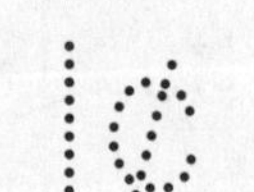 2¢ ______

Count on to find the total amount. Use coins if you need to.

1. Start with 5¢. Count on by ones.

5¢ ______ ______ ______ ______ ______

Total Amount
______

2. Start with 10¢. Count on by fives.

______ ______ ______ ______ ______

Total Amount
______

Problem Solving *Writing in Math*

3. You have 5 coins that total 23¢. Label the coins D, N, or P for dimes, nickels, or pennies.

 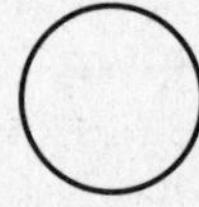 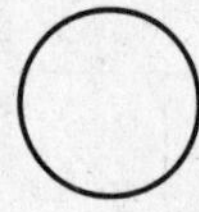  

Name ________________

Quarter and Half-Dollar

quarter
25 cents
25¢

Start with 25¢. Count on by fives.

Think: 25¢ 5¢ more 5¢ more

25¢  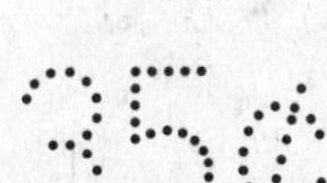

half-dollar
50 cents
50¢

Start with 50¢. Count on by tens.

Think: 50¢ 10¢ more 10¢ more

50¢  70¢

Count on to find the total amount.
Use coins if you need to.

1. Start with 25¢. Count on by tens.

25¢ ____ ____ ____ ____

Total Amount
____

2. Start with 50¢. Count on by tens and ones.

____ ____ ____ ____ ____

Total Amount
____

Problem Solving *Number Sense*

3. Draw coins so the hand holds half of 40¢.

Name ____

Counting Sets of Coins

R 3-14

To count coins, start with the coin that has the greatest value.
Count on coins from the greatest to the least value.

Find the total amount.
Draw an X on the coin with the greatest value.

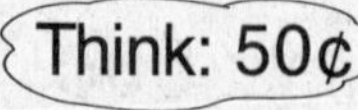

Start with 50¢. 50¢ 60¢ 70¢ 75¢

Draw an X on the coin with the greatest value.
Count on to find the total amount.

1. 

Start with ________. ________ ________ ________ ________

2. 

Start with ________. ________ ________ ________ ________

Name ______________________________

Comparing Sets of Coins

R 3-15

Which pocket has more money?
Write the total amounts in each pocket and compare them.

25¢ 30¢ 31¢ 10¢ 20¢ 21¢

31¢ (is greater than) 21¢
is less than

Write the total amounts and compare them.

1.   

_____ _____ _____ _____ _____

_____ is greater than / is less than _____

2.   

_____ _____ _____ _____ _____ _____

_____ is greater than / is less than _____

Name ______________________________

Ways to Show the Same Amount

R 3-16

You can show the same amount in different ways.

 ¢

10, 20, 30, 

31 ¢

25, 30, 31

Count on to find the total amounts.
Draw a line to the matching amount.

1. _____¢

_____, _____, _____

_____, _____, _____, _____, _____

2. _____¢

_____, _____, _____

_____, _____, _____, _____, _____, _____

3. _____¢

_____, _____, _____, _____

_____, _____, _____, _____, _____

Name ______________________________

Making Change

R 3-17

A yo-yo costs 34¢.
You pay 50¢.

To **make change,** start counting on from the price until you reach what you paid.

Start with 34¢

Count on to 50¢

Now count these coins to find the change.

34¢ 35¢ 40¢ 50¢

Your change is 16¢

Count on from the price to make change.

1. A ball costs 23¢. You pay 30¢.

   Start with ________

   Count on to ________

   23¢ ________ ________ ________

   Your change is ________

2. An action figure costs 48¢. You pay 60¢.

   Start with ________

   Count on to ________

   48¢ ________ ________ ________

   Your change is ________

Name ____________________

Dollar Bill and Dollar Coin

A **dollar bill** is equal to 100¢.
Remember to use a **dollar sign** and **decimal point** when you write $1.00.

100 pennies = **1 dollar**

100¢ = $1.00

Circle coins to show $1.00.
Write the number of coins.

1. 

_____ dimes = 1 dollar

2. 

_____ quarters = 1 dollar

3. half-dollar coins

_____ half-dollars = 1 dollar

Problem Solving *Algebra*

4. What 2 coins will make the statement true?

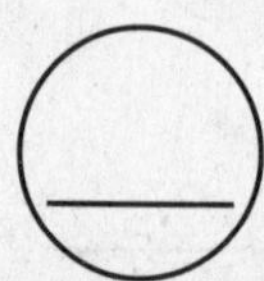
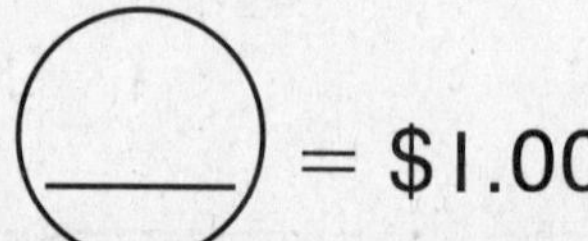
= $1.00

Name ____________________

Money, Money, Money

Long ago, coins looked very different in the United States.
Here are some old United States coins.
Count old coins the same way you count coins of today.

1794 silver dollar

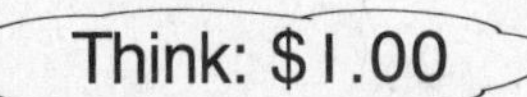

1793 copper cents

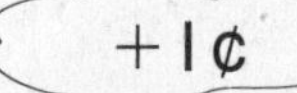

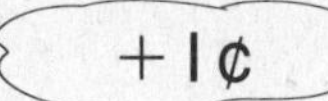

+1¢

Count on to find how much in all.

1.     

_______ _______ _______ _______ _______

2.     

_______ _______ _______ _______ _______

_______ _______

Name ______________________________

Adding Tens

R 4-1

To add tens, count on by tens.

When you add tens, only the digit in the tens place changes.

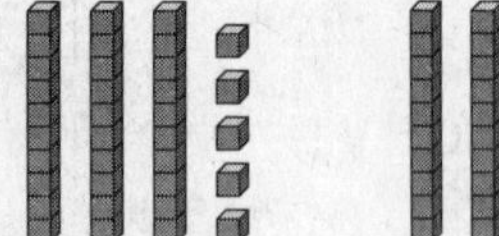

Add: 35 and 20

Think: Count on 2 tens.

35, 45, 55

So, 35 + 20 = 55.

Add tens. Use mental math or cubes.

1. 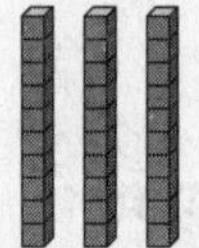

Count on 3 tens:

46, ____, ____, ____

46 and 30 = ____

46 + 30 = ____

2. 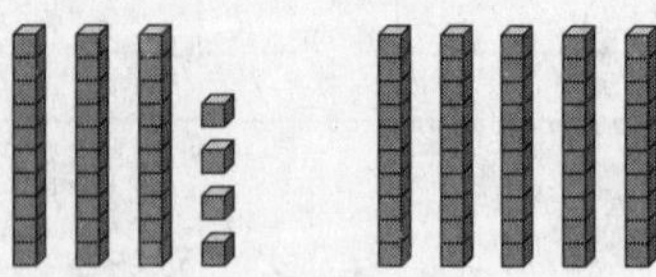

Count on 5 tens:

34, ____, ____, ____, ____, ____

34 and 50 = ____

34 + 50 = ____

3. 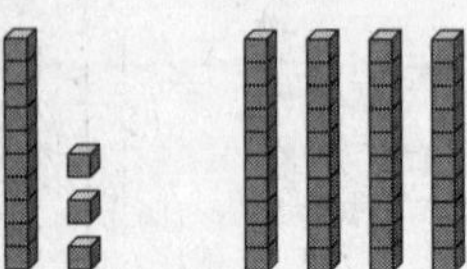

Count on 4 tens:

13, ____, ____, ____, ____

13 and 40 = ____

13 + 40 = ____

Name ___________________________________

Adding Ones

R 4-2

Add the ones to make a ten.

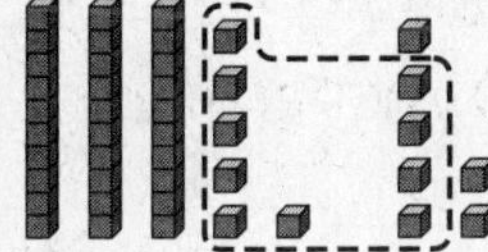

Think: 6 and 4 more make 10.

40 and 3 more make 43.

So 36 + 7 = 43.

Circle 10 ones. Then add ones. Use mental math or cubes.

1. 28 + 4 = _____

2. 47 + 8 = _____

3. 55 + 7 = _____

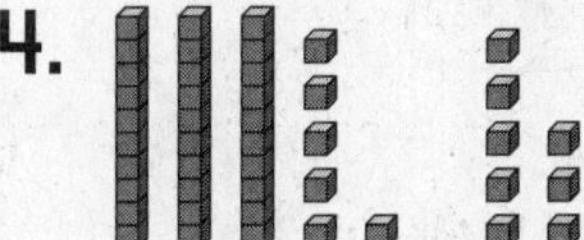

4. 36 + 8 = _____

5. 49 + 6 = _____

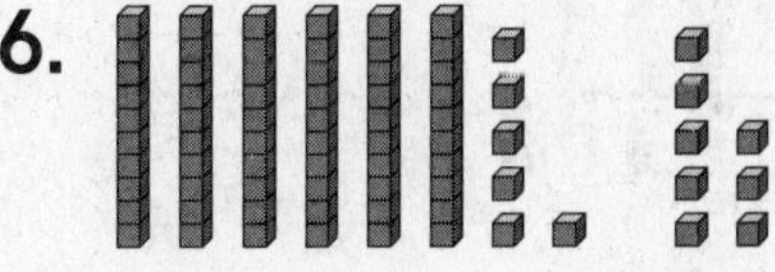

6. 66 + 8 = _____

Name ____________________

Adding Tens and Ones

R 4-3

How many cubes are there in all?

25 and 

First, count on by tens to add the tens:

Think: 25 and 3 tens

Then add the ones.

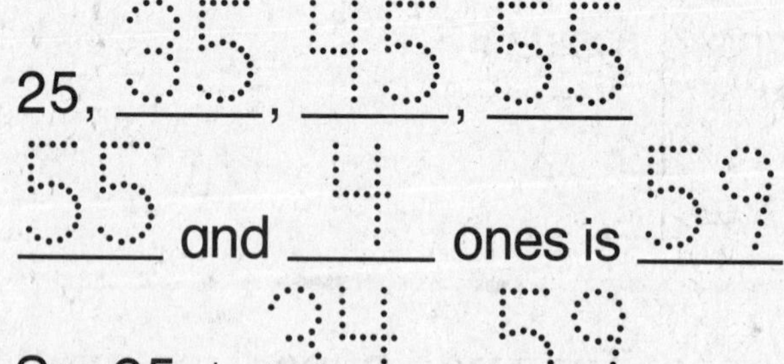

25, 35, 45, 55

55 and 4 ones is 59.

So, 25 + 34 = 59.

Add. Use mental math or cubes.

1. 34 and

34, ______, ______

54 and ______ ones is ______.

So, 34 + 25 = ______.

2. 52 and

52, ______, ______, ______

______ and ______ ones is ______.

So, 52 + ______ = ______.

3. 36 and

36, ______, ______, ______

______ and ______ ones is ______.

So, 36 + ______ = ______.

4. 11 and

11, ______, ______, ______, ______

______ and ______ ones is ______.

So, 11 + ______ = ______.

Name ____________________

Estimating Sums

R 4-4

Use mental math to **estimate.**

 and 	Think: Add the tens first. 20¢ and 10¢ is 30¢. Think: Add the ones next. 2¢ and 6¢ is 8¢ more.	You have 40¢. Do you have enough money? yes no

Estimate. Circle **yes** or **no** to answer the question.

1.  and 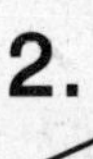 	____¢ and ____ ¢ is ____¢. ____¢ and ____¢ is ____¢ more.	You have 50¢. Do you have enough money? yes no
2. and 	____¢ and ____¢ is ____¢. ____¢ and ____¢ is ____¢ more.	You have 60¢. Do you have enough money? yes no

Name ______________________________

Subtracting Tens

R 4-5

Use tens and ones blocks to subtract tens.

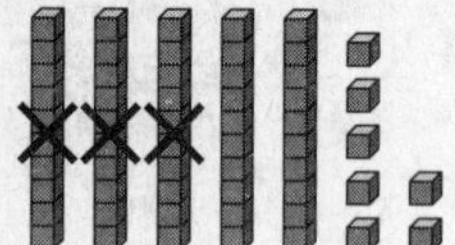

Think: Count back 3 tens.

When you subtract tens, only the digit in the tens place changes.

Subtract:

57 take away 30

57, 47, 37, 27

So, 57 − 30 = 27.

Count back to subtract tens. Use mental math or cubes.

1. 64 take away 30
Count back 3 tens.

64, _____, _____, _____

64 − 30 = _____

2. 49 take away 20
Count back 2 tens.

49, _____, _____

49 − 20 = _____

3. 72 take away 50
Count back 5 tens.

72, _____, _____, _____, _____, _____

72 − 50 = _____

Name ____________________

Subtracting Tens and Ones

R 4-6

How many are left?

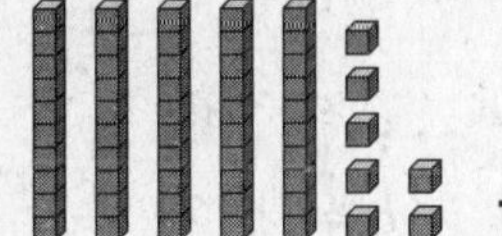 take away 31

First, count back by tens to subtract the tens.

Think: 57 take away 3 tens. 57, 47, 37, 27

Then take away the ones. 27 take away 1 one is 26.

So, 57 − 31 = 26.

I. 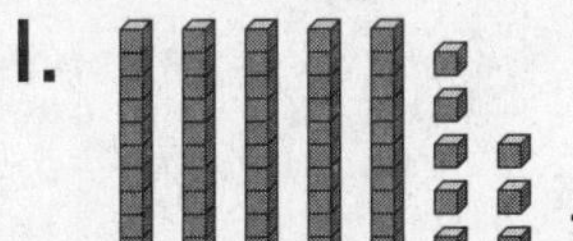 take away 26

58, ____, ____

____ take away ____ ones is ____.

____ − ____ = ____

2. 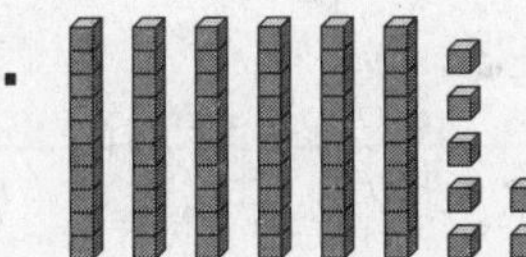 take away 43

67, ____, ____, ____, ____

____ take away ____ ones is ____.

____ − ____ = ____

Solve.

3. Pam has 59 marbles. She gives 35 marbles away. How many marbles does Pam have left?

59, ____, ____, ____

____ take away ____ ones is ____.

____ − ____ = ____

Name ________________________________

Estimating Differences

R 4-7

Use mental math to estimate.

You have 40¢.
You buy:

Will you have more or less than 20¢ left?

Think: Subtract the tens first.

40¢ − 20¢ is 20¢.

Think about the ones.

40¢ − 24¢ is more / less than 20¢.

Estimate. Circle **more** or **less** to complete each sentence.

1. You have 60¢.
   You buy:

   Will you have more or less than 30¢ left?

   60¢ − _____ ¢ is _____¢.

   _____¢ − 37¢ is more / less than 30¢.

2. You have 70¢.
   You buy:

   Will you have more or less than 20¢ left?

   70¢ − _____¢ is _____¢.

   _____¢ − 42¢ is more / less than 20¢.

Name ______________________________

PROBLEM-SOLVING STRATEGY **R 4-8**

Try, Check, and Revise

Read and Understand

Find two numbers with a sum of 28.

12	15	16

Plan and Solve

Try: Find the ones digits that add up to 8.

Check: 12 and 15

2 ones + 5 ones = 7 ones

Revise: 15 and 16

5 ones + 6 ones = 11 ones

Revise: 12 and 16

2 ones + 6 ones = 8 ones

Now check the tens digits for 12 and 16.

1 ten + 1 ten = 2 tens

Look Back and Check

So

12 ones + 16 ones = 28

Does your answer make sense?

Find pairs of numbers with the given sum.

1. Find numbers with a sum of 37.

16	15	21

Try: Find the ones digits that add up to 7.

Check: 16 and 15

___ ones + ___ ones = ___ ones

Revise: 15 and 21

___ ones + ___ one = ___ ones

Revise: 16 and 21

___ ones + ___ one = ___ ones

Now check the tens digits.

___ ten + ___ tens = ___ tens

So

___ and ___ is 37.

Name ______________________

Addition and Subtraction Patterns

R 4-9

Find the numbers in the pattern:

7, 17, 27, 37, 47, 57, 67, 77

1	2	3	4	5	6	7	8	9	10
11	12	13	14	15	16	17	18	19	20
21	22	23	24	25	26	27	28	29	30
31	32	33	34	35	36	37	38	39	40
41	42	43	44	45	46	47	48	49	50
51	52	53	54	55	56	57	58	59	60
61	62	63	64	65	66	67	68	69	70
71	72	73	74	75	76	77	78	79	80
81	82	83	84	85	86	87	88	89	90
91	92	93	94	95	96	97	98	99	100

Look at the ones digit.
It is 7 each time.

Look at the tens digit.
It goes up 1 each time.

The pattern is add 10.

Find the pattern.

1. Color these numbers on the hundred chart:
   4, 9, 14, 19, 24, 29, 34, 39.

   Look at the ones. The ones pattern is ______________

   Look at the tens. The tens pattern is ______________

   The pattern is ______________.

2. Color these numbers on the hundred chart:
   71, 73, 75, 77, 79, 81, 83, 85, 87, 89.

   Look at the ones. The ones pattern is ______________

   Look at the tens. The tens pattern is ______________

   The pattern is ______________.

Name ______________________________

Finding Parts of 100

R 4-10

Find parts for 100.

Draw more tens to make 100.

Think: Count up to make 100.

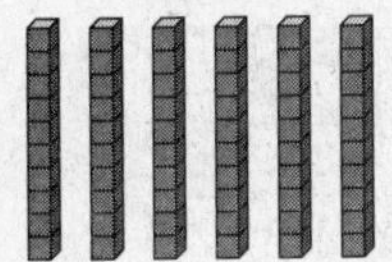

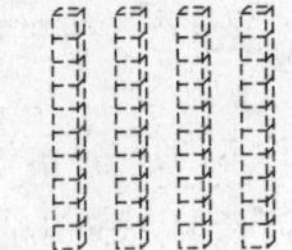

60 and 10 is 70.
70 and 10 is 80.
80 and 10 is 90.
90 and 10 is 100.

60 and __40__ is 100.

Now draw tens and ones to make 100.

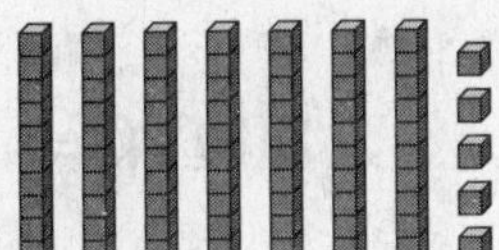

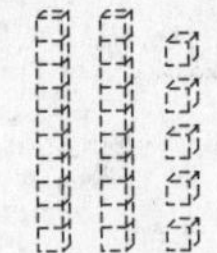

75 and 10 is 85.
85 and 10 is 95.
95 and 5 is 100.

75 and __25__ is 100.

Draw tens to find the other part of 100.

1. 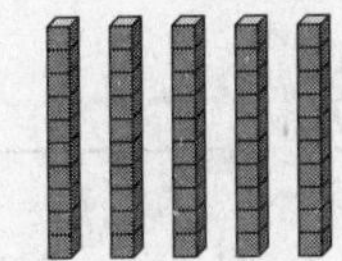

50 and _____ is 100.

Draw tens and ones to make 100. Count up.

2. 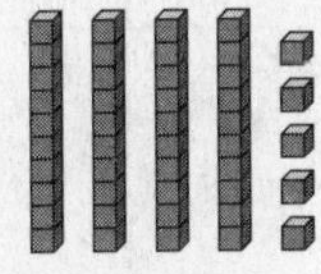

45 and _____ is 100.

3. 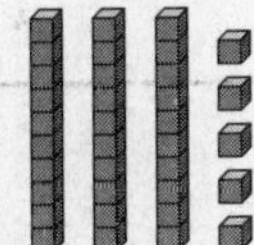

35 and _____ is 100.

Name ______________________________

PROBLEM-SOLVING SKILL **R 4-11**

Look Back and Check

Pat has 42 stamps.
He gets 20 more stamps.

Now Pat has (62) / 22 stamps.

Check

Think: Which number makes sense?

Pat gets 20 more stamps.

62 is more than 42.

22 is less than 42.

So, Pat has (62) / 22 stamps.

Circle the number that makes sense.
Check if your answer should be more or less.

1. Eric has 67 marbles.
He gives 20 marbles away.

Now Eric has 87 / 47 marbles.

Check

Eric gives 20 marbles ________.

87 is ____________ than 67.

47 is ____________ than 67.

2. Mary has 25 flowers.
She picks 10 more flowers.

Now Mary has 35 / 15 flowers.

Check

Mary ________ 10 more flowers.

35 is ____________ than 25.

15 is ____________ than 25.

Name ______________________________

PROBLEM-SOLVING APPLICATIONS **R 4-12**

Take Me Out to the Ball Game!

Use the chart to answer the questions.

Innings	1	2	3	4	5	6	7	8	9	Final Score
Green Team	3	2	4	5	3	1	2	4	2	26
Blue Team	1	2	2	4	3	1	1	2	1	17

How many more runs were scored by the Green Team than the Blue Team in the first inning?

Write a subtraction sentence to compare.

3 – 1 = 2 more runs

How many runs in all were scored in the 3rd inning?

Write an addition sentence to find out how many in all.

4 + 2 = 6 runs

Add or subtract.

1. How many more runs were scored by the Green Team than the Blue Team?

   ____ ◯ ____ = ____ more runs

2. How many runs were scored by the Blue Team in the 3rd and 4th innings?

   ____ ◯ ____ = ____ runs

Name ______________________________

Adding With and Without Regrouping

R 5-1

Add 37 + 6.

Show 37.

Tens	Ones
3 tens	7 ones

Add the ones.

Tens	Ones
3 tens	7 ones + 6 ones

7 + 6 = 13

There are more than 10 ones.

Do you need to regroup?

(Yes) No

Regroup. Add.

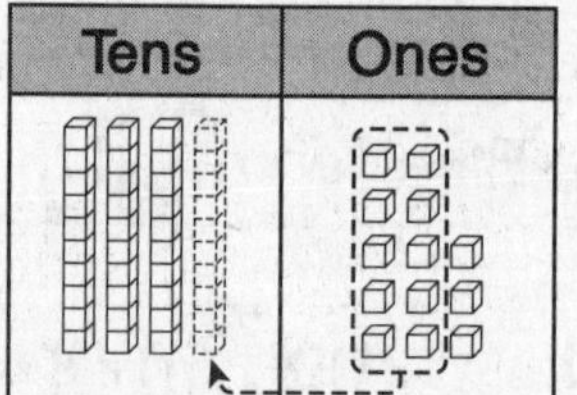

37 + 6 = 43

Use cubes and Workmat 4. Add. Regroup if you need to.

1. Show 28.

Tens	Ones
2 tens	8 ones

Add 4.

Tens	Ones
2 tens	8 ones + 4 ones

8 + 4 = ______

Do you need to regroup?

Yes No

Regroup. Add.

Tens	Ones
2 tens + 1 ten	12 ones

28 + 4 = ______

2. Show 26.

Tens	Ones
2 tens	6 ones

Add 9.

Tens	Ones
2 tens	6 ones + 9 ones

6 + 9 = ______

Do you need to regroup?

Yes No

Regroup. Add.

Tens	Ones
2 tens + 1 ten	15 ones

26 + 9 = ______

Name ______________________________

Recording Addition

R 5-2

Add 35 + 7.

Step 1:
How many ones?

5 + 7 = 12

Tens	Ones
3 tens	12 ones

	Tens	Ones
	☐	
	3	5
+		7
		2

Step 2:
Regroup 12 as
1 ten and 2 ones.
Write 2 ones.

	Tens	Ones
	1	
	3	5
+		7
		2

Step 3:
How many tens?

3 + 1 = 4 tens

	Tens	Ones
	1	
	3	5
+		7
	4	2

So, 35 + 7 = 42.

Use cubes and Workmat 4. Add.
Did you need to regroup? Circle **yes** or **no.**

	Tens	Ones
	☐	
	4	6
+		9

yes no

	Tens	Ones
	☐	
	5	2
+		7

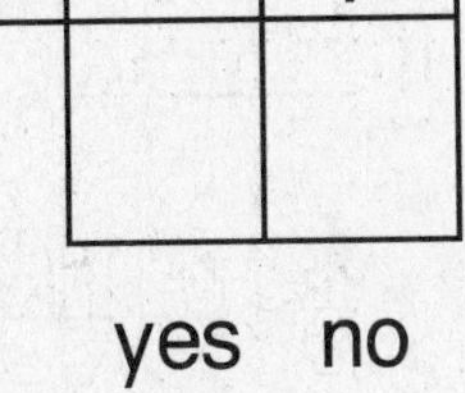

yes no

	Tens	Ones
	☐	
	3	8
+		5

yes no

	Tens	Ones
	☐	
	6	7
+		3

yes no

Name ______________________________

Adding Two-Digit Numbers With and Without Regrouping

R 5-3

Add 46 + 18.

Step 1:
How many ones?

6 + 8 = 14

Tens	Ones
5 tens	14 ones

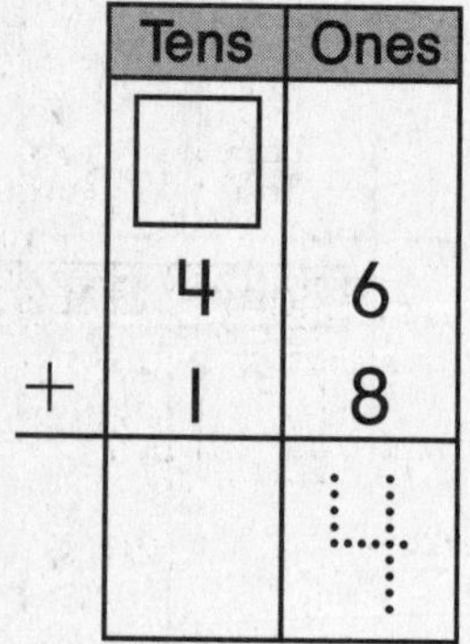

Step 2:
Do I need to regroup?

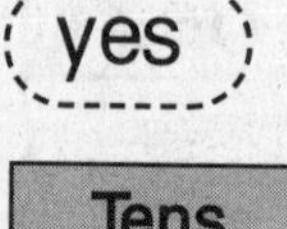

yes   no

Tens	Ones
6 tens	4 ones

	Tens	Ones
	1	
	4	6
+	1	8
		4

Step 3:
How many tens?

5 + 1 = 6 tens

Tens	Ones
6 tens	4 ones

	Tens	Ones
	1	
	4	6
+	1	8
	6	4

So, 46 + 18 = 64.

Use cubes and Workmat 4. Add.

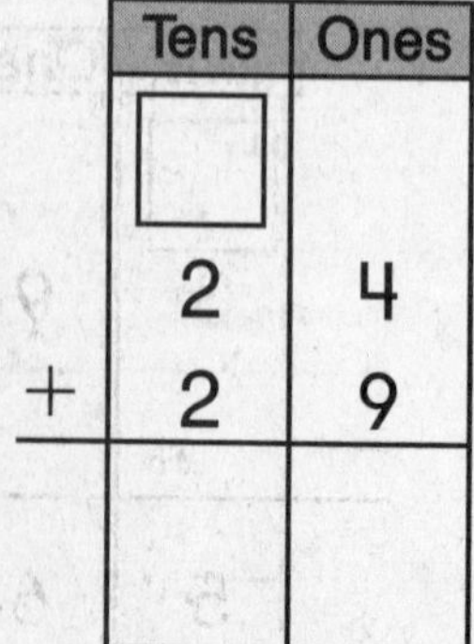

	Tens	Ones
	☐	
	5	2
+	1	7

	Tens	Ones
	☐	
	3	8
+	4	5

	Tens	Ones
	☐	
	1	7
+	6	3

Name ______________________

Practice With Two-Digit Addition

R 5-4

Remember the steps for adding:

Step 1: Add the ones. **Step 2:** Regroup if you need to. **Step 3:** Add the tens.

34 + 27 = ?

Regroup 11 ones as 1 ten and 1 one.

	Tens	Ones
	1	
	3	4
+	2	7
	6	1

12 + 36 = ?

You do not need to regroup 8 ones.

	Tens	Ones
	1	2
+	3	6
	4	8

Write the addition problem. Find the sum.

1\. 15 + 26

	Tens	Ones
	1	5
+	2	6

32 + 24

	Tens	Ones
	3	2
+	2	

28 + 15

	Tens	Ones
	2	8
+		

49 + 13

	Tens	Ones
+		

Problem Solving *Algebra*

2\. Begin with 39. Find the number that gives you a sum of 56. Use cubes to help.

The number is ______.

	Tens	Ones
	3	9
+		
	5	6

Name ____

Adding Money

R 5-5

Adding money is the same as adding two-digit numbers.

Add two-digit numbers.

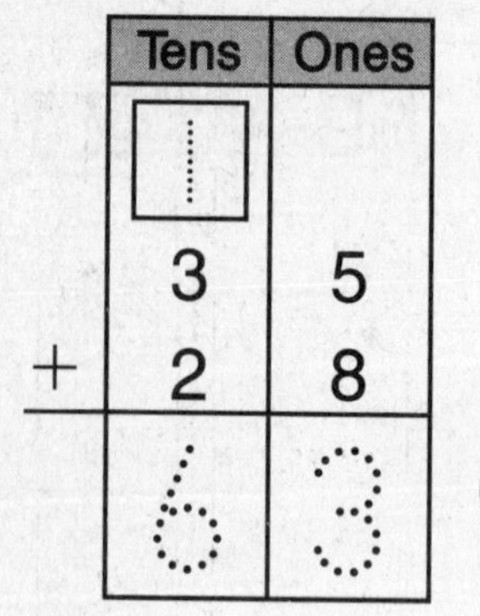

	Tens	Ones
	1	
	3	5
+	2	8
	6	3

Add money.

	Tens	Ones
	1	
	3	5¢
+	2	8¢
	6	3¢

Remember to write the ¢ sign in your answer.

Add to find the total amount.

1.

	Tens	Ones
	☐	
	1	8
+	4	7

	Tens	Ones
	☐	
	1	8¢
+	4	7¢

2.

	Tens	Ones
	☐	
	3	3
+	2	5

	Tens	Ones
	☐	
	3	3¢
+	2	5¢

Problem Solving *Visual Thinking*

3. Sarah spends 25¢ on an apple. Sarah has 60¢. Does she have enough ¢ to buy juice for 39¢ too? Circle **yes** or **no**.

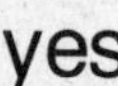

yes no

_____¢

Name ______________________________

Adding Three Numbers

R 5-6

Remember you can add in any order. Try different ways to add.

Look for doubles facts.
Add the doubles first.

```
  14
  35   4 + 4 = 8
+ 24
  73   8 + 5 = 13
```

Count on 1, 2, or 3.

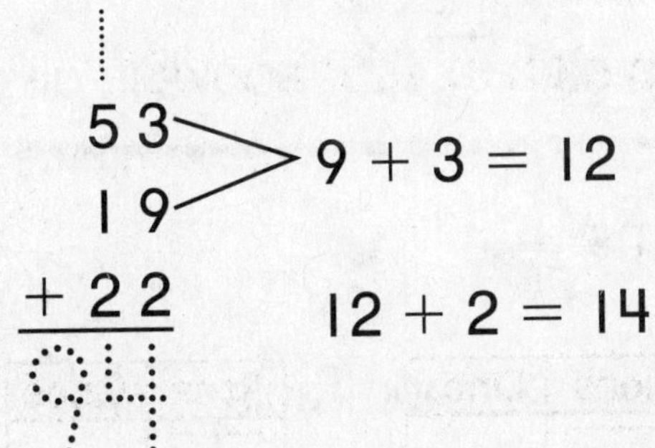

Make a ten fact.
Look for a ten first.

```
  13
  26   6 + 4 = 10
+ 24
  63   10 + 3 = 13
```

1. Add.
Look for doubles.

```
  11        26
  35        22
+ 25      + 16
```

2. Add.
Count on.

```
  32        40
  17        29
+ 24      + 12
```

3. Add.
Make a ten.

```
  15        17
  28        23
+ 22      + 12
```

Name ____________________

PROBLEM-SOLVING SKILL **R 5-7**

Use Data from a Table

This table shows data about how many animal books are in the library.

Use data from the table to solve problems.

Animal Books in the Library	
Kinds of Books	**Number of Books**
Mammals	42
Birds	28
Insects	14
Reptiles	33

How many books about birds and insects are there in all?

Do I add or subtract?

What numbers do I use in the chart?

Birds: 28 books
Insects: 14 books
Add to find how many in all.

$$\begin{array}{r} 28 \\ +\ 14 \\ \hline 42 \end{array}$$

42 books in all

Use data from the table to solve the problems.

1. How many books about mammals and reptiles are there in all?

   ____ mammals
   \+ ____ reptiles
   ____ books in all

   What numbers do I use?

2. How many books about birds and reptiles are there in all?

   ____ birds
   \+ ____ reptiles
   ____ books in all

   What numbers do I use?

3. How many books about birds, insects, and reptiles are there in all? ____ books in all

Name ____________________

Estimating Sums

R 5-8

Remember when you estimate, you find the closest ten.

Estimate 22 + 37.

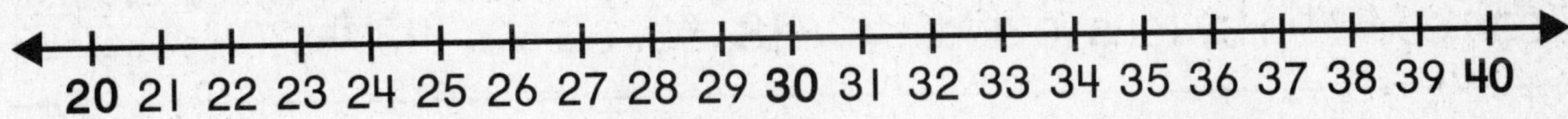

Step 1: Find the closest ten.

22
+ 37

22 is closest to 20.

37 is closest to 40.

Step 2: Estimate.

22 is about 20.
37 is about + 40.

22 + 37 is about 60.

Step 3: Add.

22
+ 37
59

22 + 37 = 59

Estimate the sum. Then solve and compare.

Find the closest ten. | Estimate. | Solve.

1. 18 + 34

18 is about ____.

34 is about ____.

18
+ 34

18 is closest to ____.

34 is closest to ____.

18 + 34 is about ____.

18 + 34 = ____

---

2. 42 + 13

42 is about ____.

13 is about ____.

42
+ 13

42 is closest to ____.

13 is closest to ____.

42 + 13 is about ____.

42 + 13 = ____

Name ______________________________

Ways to Add

R 5-9

Use **mental math** to add.

43 + 20

I can count up by tens to add. → 43, 53, 63 → 43 + 20 = 63

Use **cubes** to add.

27 + 18

Regroup 10 ones for one ten. → 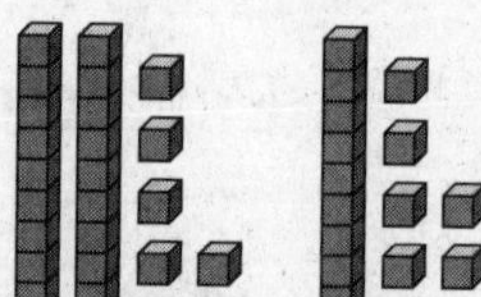 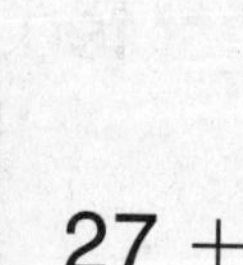 27 + 18 = 45

Use **paper and pencil** to add.

45 + 15

```
  1
  45
+ 15
   0
```

Write 1 ten over the tens column. → 45 + 15 = 60

Use a **calculator** to add.

56 + 29 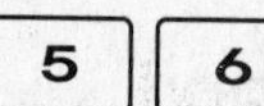  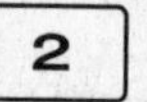 56 + 29 = 85

Circle the best way to solve the problem. Then add.

1. 73 + 18 — mental math / calculator

2. 46 + 30 — mental math / paper and pencil

3. 54 + 17 — mental math / cubes

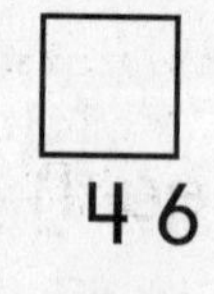

4. 34 + 23 — mental math / paper and pencil

Name ________________________________

PROBLEM-SOLVING STRATEGY **R 5-10**

Try, Check, and Revise

Read and Understand

Animal Stickers	
Animal	**Cost**
Elephant	33¢
Lion	18¢
Tiger	25¢
Zebra	21¢

Ken collects animal stickers.
He paid 43¢ for two stickers.
Which stickers did he choose?

Find two stickers that add up to 43¢.

Plan and Solve

First, pick two numbers: → 25¢ and 21¢
Next, add the numbers: → 25¢ + 21¢ = 46¢
Compare the numbers: → 46¢ does not equal 43¢.

Try again. Pick 18¢ and 25¢. → 18¢ + 25¢ = 43

So, Ken chose the lion and tiger stickers.

Look Back and Check

Are there other pairs of stickers you should check?

Try and check to solve each problem.

1. Nina paid 51¢ for two stickers.
   Which stickers did she choose?

   ____________ and ____________ stickers

2. Keesha paid 46¢ for two stickers.
   Which stickers did she choose?

   ____________ and ____________ stickers

Name ______________________________

PROBLEM-SOLVING APPLICATIONS **R 5-11**

The Wonderful World of Plants

There are 26 plants in one patch.
There are 17 plants in another patch.
How many plants are there in all?

Add to find how many in all.

Step 1: Add the ones. Regroup.

```
 [1]
  26
+ 17
----
   3
```

Remember to regroup 10 ones as 1 ten if needed.

Step 2: Add the tens.

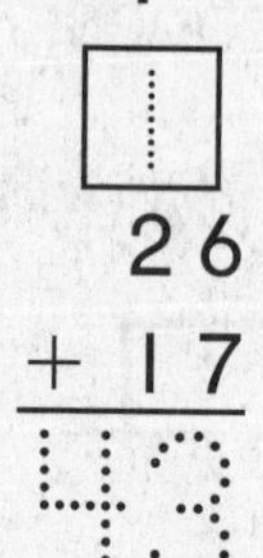

Solve.

1. One Venus's-flytrap plant has 15 traps.
Another Venus's-flytrap plant has 19 traps.
How many traps do the plants have in all?

_____ ◯ _____ = _____ plants in all

2. One group of plants catches 23 insects.
Another group of plants catches 16 insects.
How many insects are caught in all?

_____ ◯ _____ = _____ insects in all

3. If 17 insects got stuck on one plant,
and 9 insects got stuck on another plant,
and 5 insects got stuck on a third plant,
how many insects in all would be stuck?

_____ ◯ _____ ◯ _____ = _____ insects in all

Name ____________________

Subtracting With and Without Regrouping

R 6-1

Subtract 7 from 42.

Show 42.

Tens	Ones

There are not enough ones to subtract 7.

Regroup.

Tens	Ones

I ten becomes 10 ones.

Subtract 7 ones.

Tens	Ones

Do you need to regroup?

(Yes) No

12 − 7 = 5 ones

42 − 7 = 35

Put cubes on Workmat 4.
Subtract. Regroup if you need to.

I. Subtract 5 from 31.

Show 31.

Tens	Ones

Regroup.

Tens	Ones

Subtract 5 ones.

Tens	Ones

Do you need to regroup?

No

11 − 5 = 6 ones.

31 − 5 = ____

Name ____

Recording Subtraction

R 6-2

Subtract 8 from 52.

Step 1
Think: There are not enough ones to subtract 8.

Tens	Ones
5 tens	2 ones

	Tens	Ones
	☐	☐
	5	2
−		8

Step 2
Regroup 1 ten as 10 ones.
Write 12 ones.
$12 - 8 = 4$ ones

Tens	Ones
4 tens	12 ones

	Tens	Ones
	4	12
	~~5~~	~~2~~
−		8
		4

Step 3
Subtract the tens.
$4 - 0 = 4$ tens

Tens	Ones
4 tens	4 ones (8 crossed out)

	Tens	Ones
	4	12
	~~5~~	~~2~~
−		8
	4	4

So, $52 - 8 =$ 44.

Put cubes on Workmat 4. Subtract.
Did you need to regroup? Circle **yes** or **no**.

1.

	Tens	Ones
	☐	☐
	4	3
−		9

yes no

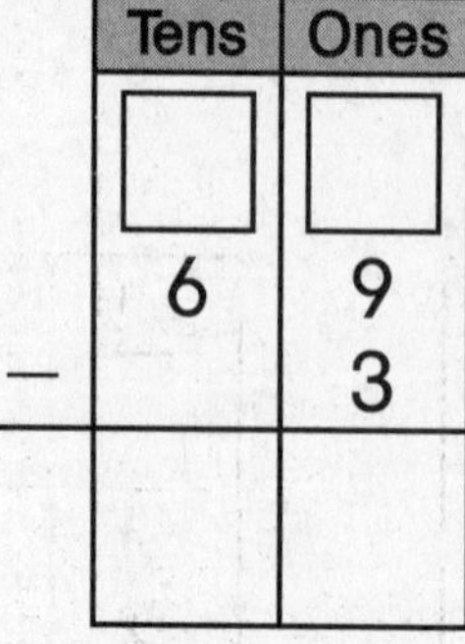

yes no

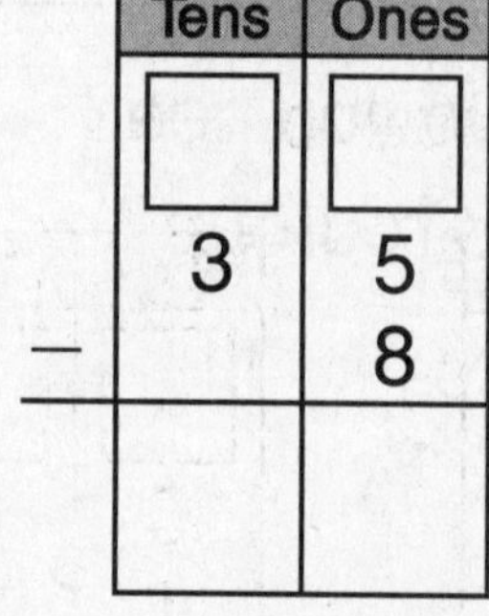

yes no

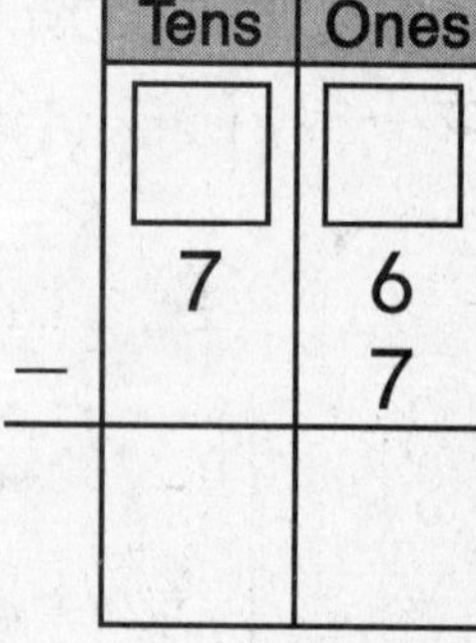

yes no

Name ______________________________

R 6-3

Subtracting Two-Digit Numbers With and Without Regrouping

Subtract 16 from 43.

Step 1
Think: There are not enough ones to subtract 6.

Tens	Ones
☐	☐
4	3
− 1	6

Step 2
Think: Do I need to regroup?

13 − 6 = 7 ones

Tens	Ones
3	13
~~4~~	~~3~~
− 1	6
	7

Step 3
Think: Subtract the tens.

3 − 1 = 2 tens

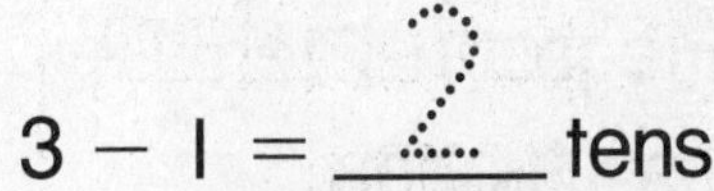

Tens	Ones
3	13
~~4~~	~~3~~
− 1	6
2	7

So, 43 − 16 = 27.

Put cubes on Workmat 4. Subtract.
Regroup if you need to.

1.

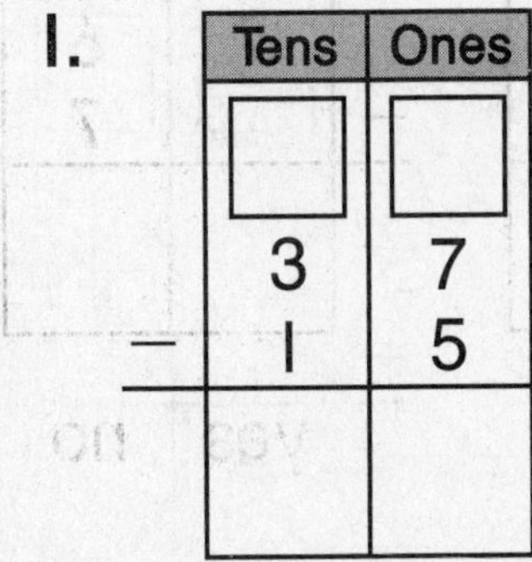

Tens	Ones
☐	☐
3	7
− 1	5

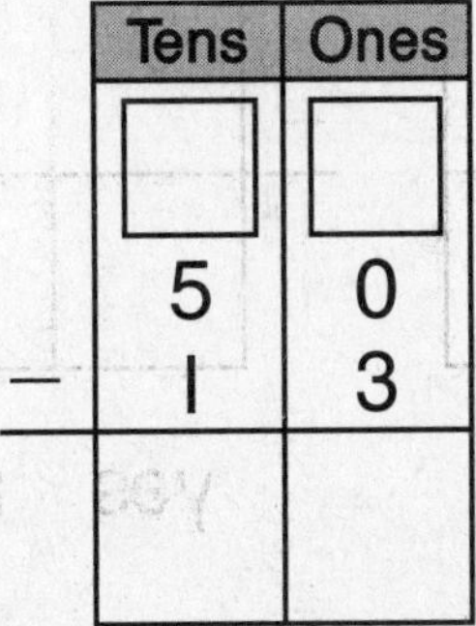

Tens	Ones
☐	☐
5	0
− 1	3

Tens	Ones
☐	☐
7	6
− 2	8

Tens	Ones
☐	☐
4	5
− 2	7

Name ______________________________

Practice with Two-Digit Subtraction

R 6-4

Remember the steps for subtracting:

Step 1: Look at the ones.
Regroup if you need to.

Step 2: Subtract the ones.
Subtract the tens.

54 − 17
Regroup 1 ten as 10 ones.

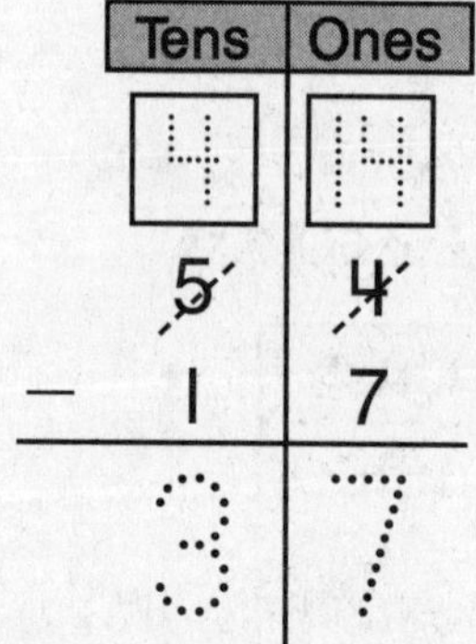

38 − 13
You do **not** need to regroup 8 ones.
Subtract the ones and tens.

Tens	Ones
3	8
− 1	3
2	5

Remember the steps for subtracting. Find the difference.

1. 64 − 18

Tens	Ones
6	4
− 1	8

37 − 14

Tens	Ones
3	7
− 1	4

45 − 26

Tens	Ones
4	5
− 2	6

73 − 25

Tens	Ones
7	3
− 1	5

Problem Solving *Number Sense*

2. Use each number once.
Make the smallest sum.

5 3 2 4

Tens	Ones
+	

Name ____________________

PROBLEM-SOLVING STRATEGY **R 6-5**

Write a Number Sentence

Read and Understand

Sue has 42 flowers. She gives 15 flowers to her sister. How many flowers are left?

Plan and Solve

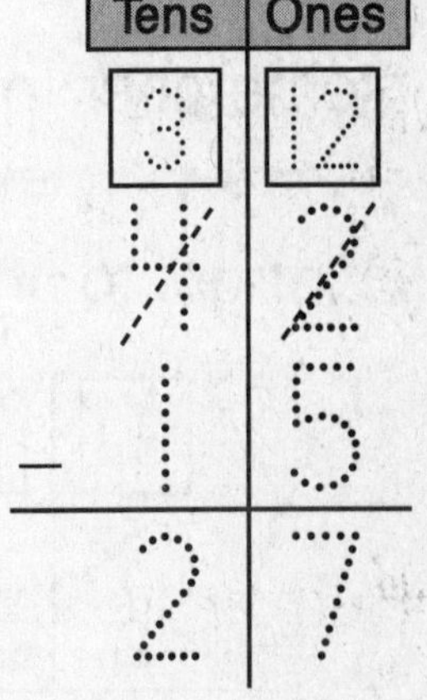

Look for clue words to decide whether to add or subtract. "How many are left" tells you to subtract. "How many in all" tells you to add.

Write a number sentence. Use the numbers in the problem.

42 − 15 = 27 flowers left

Write a number sentence to solve the problem.

1. Paul has 37 marbles. He gives 18 marbles to a friend. How many marbles are left?

Tens	Ones

____ ◯ ____ ◯ ____ marbles left.

2. Tina has 23 crayons. She gets 27 more crayons. How many crayons does Tina have in all?

Tens	Ones

____ ◯ ____ ◯ ____ crayons.

Name ____________________

Subtracting Money

Subtracting money is the same as subtracting two-digit numbers.

$$\begin{array}{r} 51¢ \\ -\ 22¢ \\ \hline \end{array}$$

Think of the pennies as ones and the dimes as tens.

	Tens	Ones
	4	11
	5	1 ¢
−	2	2 ¢
	2	9 ¢

Remember to write the cents sign in your answer.

Subtract to find the difference.

1.

	Tens	Ones		Tens	Ones		Tens	Ones		Tens	Ones
	5	9 ¢		6	5 ¢		7	3 ¢		4	2 ¢
−	2	4 ¢	−	2	4 ¢	−	5	7 ¢	−	2	8 ¢

2.

	Tens	Ones		Tens	Ones		Tens	Ones		Tens	Ones
	8	0 ¢		7	2 ¢		6	0 ¢		4	8 ¢
−	2	9 ¢	−	3	6 ¢	−	4	8 ¢	−	1	8 ¢

Problem Solving *Reasoning*

3. Greg has 58¢. He spends 25¢.
How much money does Greg have left?

Greg has ______ left.

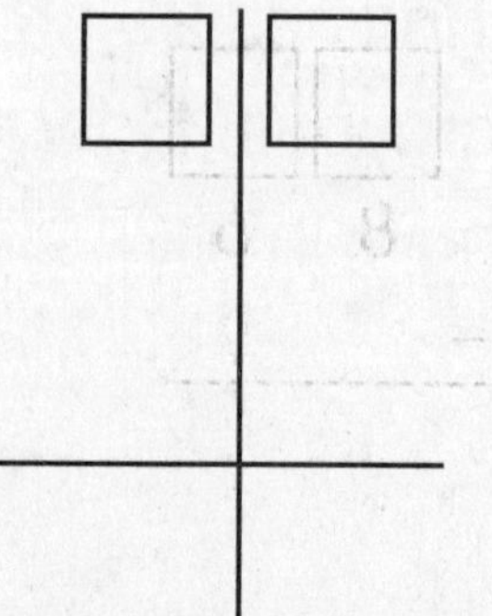

Name ______________________________

Using Addition to Check Subtraction

R 6-7

When you subtract,
you start with the whole.
Then you take part away.
The other part is left.

$$\begin{array}{r} 37 \\ -\ 12 \\ \hline 25 \end{array}$$

Tens	Ones

To check your work,
put the 2 parts back together.
Add. Your answer should be
the whole you started with.

$$\begin{array}{r} 25 \\ +\ 12 \\ \hline 37 \end{array}$$

Tens	Ones
and	and

Subtract.
Check your answer by adding.

1. $$\begin{array}{r} 5\ 4 \\ -\ 1\ 9 \\ \hline \end{array}$$

2. 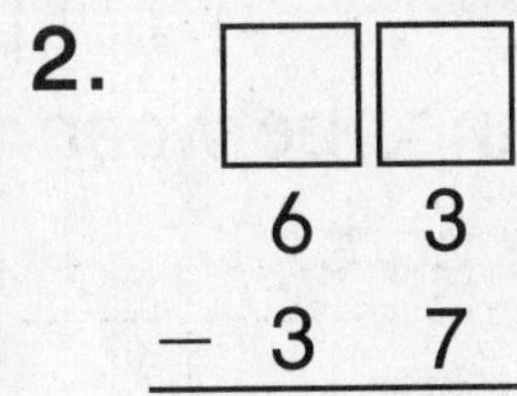

$$\begin{array}{r} 6\ 3 \\ -\ 3\ 7 \\ \hline \end{array}$$

3. $$\begin{array}{r} 8\ 6 \\ -\ \ \ 9 \\ \hline \end{array}$$

4. $$\begin{array}{r} 3\ 3 \\ -\ 2\ 1 \\ \hline \end{array}$$

Name ___________________________

Estimating Differences

Remember, when you estimate, you find the closest 10.
Estimate the difference between 49 and 32.

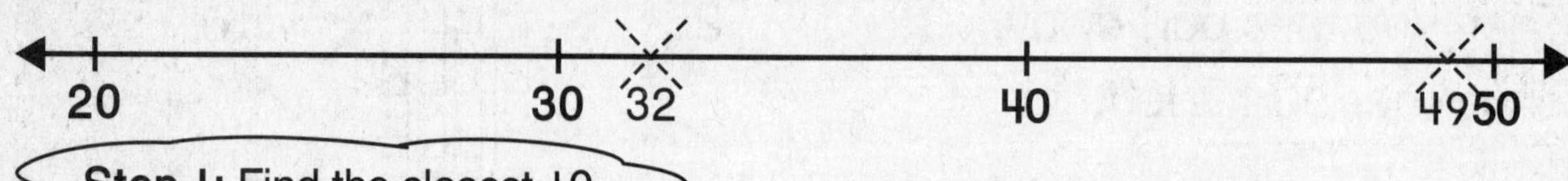

Step 1: Find the closest 10.

Find 49 on the number line. 49 is closest to 50.

Find 32 on the number line. 32 is closest to 30.

Step 2: Estimate.

$$\begin{array}{r} 50 \\ -\ 30 \\ \hline 20 \end{array}$$

Step 3: Solve.

$$\begin{array}{r} 49 \\ -\ 32 \\ \hline 17 \end{array}$$

49 − 32 is about 20.

Estimate the difference between 63 and 24.
Then solve and compare.

1. Find the closest ten.

63 is closest to ____.

24 is closest to ____.

63 − 24 is about ____.

Estimate.

− ______

Solve.

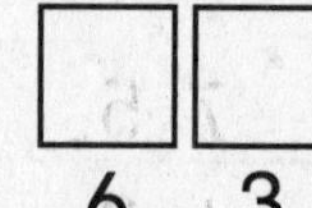

$$\begin{array}{r} 6\ 3 \\ -\ 2\ 4 \\ \hline \end{array}$$

Name ____________________

Ways to Subtract

R 6-9

Remember there are 4 ways you can subtract.

Use **mental math** to subtract. 75 − 20

Think: Count back 2 tens to subtract. 75, 65, 55 75 − 20 = 55

Use **cubes** to subtract. 38 − 12

Show 38. Take away 1 ten.
Then take away 2 ones.

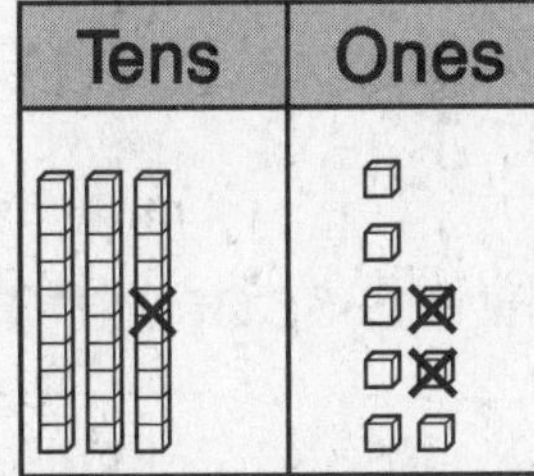

38 − 12 = 26

Use **paper and pencil** to subtract. 60 − 23

Think: Regroup 1 ten as 10 ones.

```
 [5] [10]
  6   0
− 2   3
```

60 − 23 = 37

Use a **calculator** to subtract. 85 − 59

Press 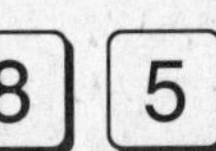   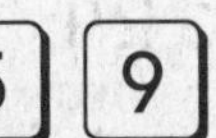 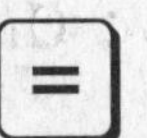

85 − 59 = 26

Circle the better way to solve the problem. Then subtract.

1. 75 − 10 = ____ paper and pencil / mental math

2. 49 − 22 = ____ cubes / mental math

3. 67 − 19 = ____ mental math / paper and pencil

4. 83 − 30 = ____ calculator / mental math

Name ______________________________

PROBLEM-SOLVING SKILL **R 6-10**

Extra Information

Sometimes there is extra information that you do not need to answer the question.

There are 4 children on a bowling team. Mike bowls a score of 65. Sherry bowls a score of 33. How much higher is Mike's score?

What is the question asking?

How much higher is Mike's score than Sherry's score?

Which information do you need to answer the question?

Mike bowls a score of 65. Sherry bowls a score of 33.

Which information doesn't tell about the scores?

There are 4 children on a bowling team.

$$\begin{array}{r} 65 \\ -\ 33 \\ \hline 32 \end{array}$$

32 points higher

Cross out the extra information. Then solve the problem. Solve

1. There are 78 adults at the bowling alley.
   There are 39 children at the bowling alley.
   Mark bowls a score of 82.
   How many more adults than children are there?

   _____ more adults

2. In the first game, Sari bowls a score of 57.
   Her brother bowls a score of 48.
   In the second game, Sari bowls a score of 38.
   What is Sari's total score for the two games?

   _____ points

Name ______________________________

PROBLEM-SOLVING APPLICATIONS **R 6-11**

Here Kitty, Kitty!

Subtract to **compare numbers.**

A mother lion has 30 teeth.
Her baby cub has only 14 teeth.
How many more teeth does the mother lion have?

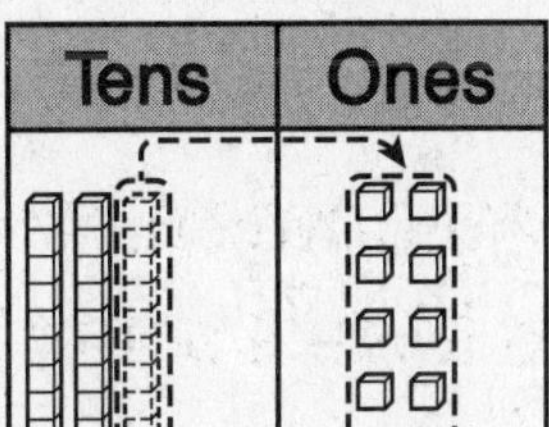

Subtract.

Tens	Ones

Step 1
Regroup. Subtract the ones.

$$\begin{array}{r} \overset{2}{\not{3}}\,\overset{10}{\not{0}} \\ -\ 1\ 4 \\ \hline 6 \end{array}$$

Step 2
Subtract the tens.

$$\begin{array}{r} \overset{2}{\not{3}}\,\overset{10}{\not{0}} \\ -\ 1\ 4 \\ \hline 1\ 6 \end{array}$$

Solve. Show your work.

1. A tiger is 87 inches long. A lion is 76 inches long. How much longer is the tiger than the lion? _____ inches longer

2. There are 27 lions in a pride. 9 of the lions are cubs. How many adult lions are in the pride? _____ adult lions

3. There are 17 lions in a group. 10 lions leave the group. How many lions are left? _____ lions are left.

Name ____________________

Flat Surfaces, Vertices, and Edges

R 7-1

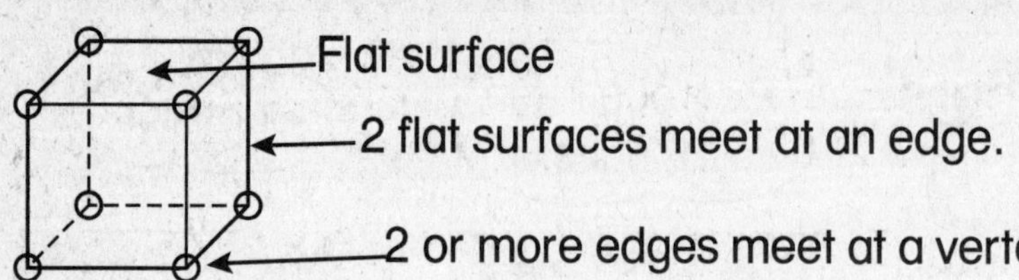

A cube has __6__ flat surfaces.

A cube has __12__ edges.

A cube has __8__ vertices.

A cube has the same shape as a .

Circle the object with the same shape.
Write how many flat surfaces, vertices, and edges.
Use solid figures to help you.

1. 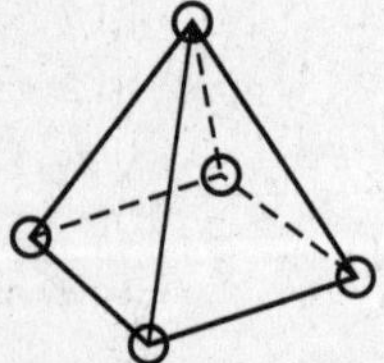  

A pyramid has ____ flat surfaces, ____ vertices, and ____ edges.

2. 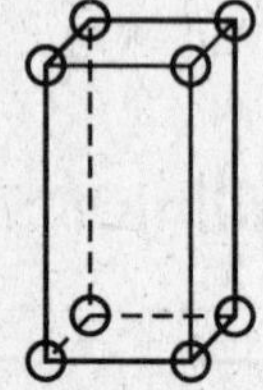 

A rectangular prism has ____ flat surfaces, ____ vertices,

and ____ edges.

Name ______________________________

Relating Plane Shapes to Solid Figures

R 7-2

If you trace the flat surfaces of this box, you will get these shapes.

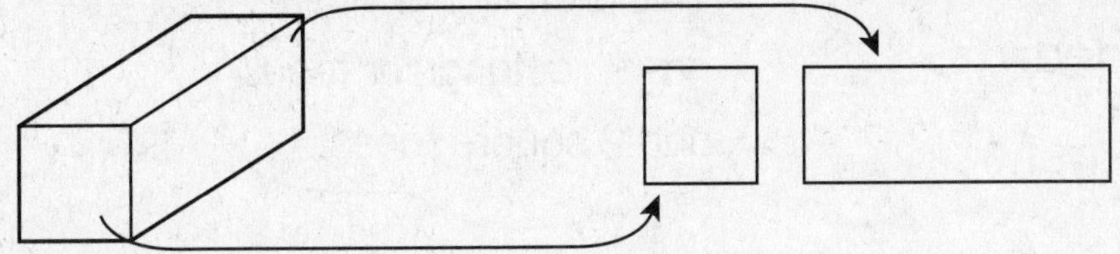

Use the solid figures in your classroom.

Trace one flat surface. Draw the shape on the page.

1. 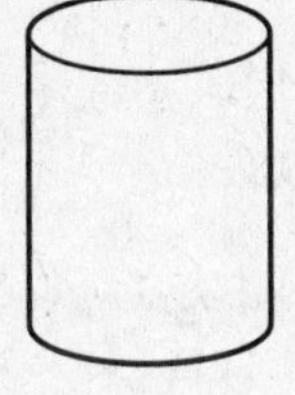	
2. 	
3. 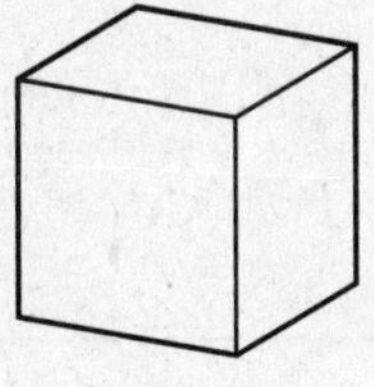	
4. 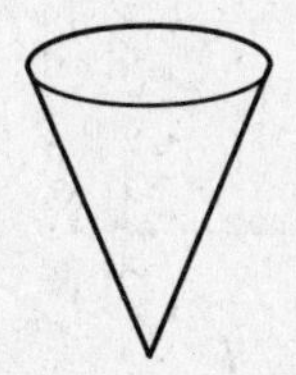	

Name ____________________

PROBLEM-SOLVING SKILL **R 7-3**

Use Data from a Picture

A net is a pattern that makes a solid figure when folded.

Count the faces of the net.

This rectangular prism has 4 rectangular faces and 2 square faces.

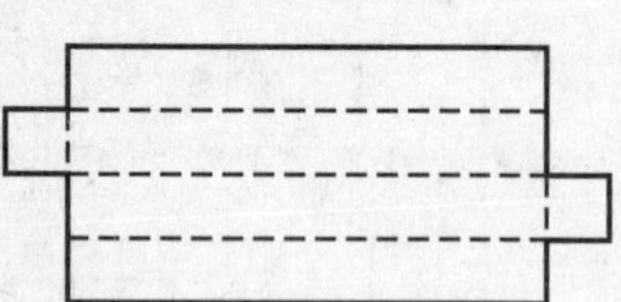

It has __4__ rectangular faces

and __2__ square faces.

Circle the solid figure that this net would make when folded.

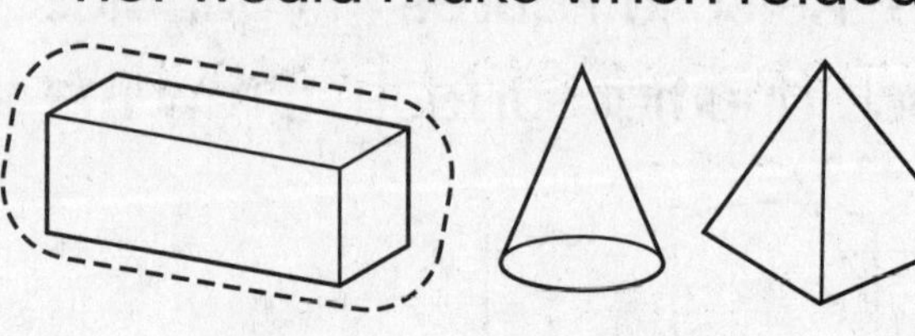

Circle the solid figure that the net makes when folded. Use the clues to help you.

1.

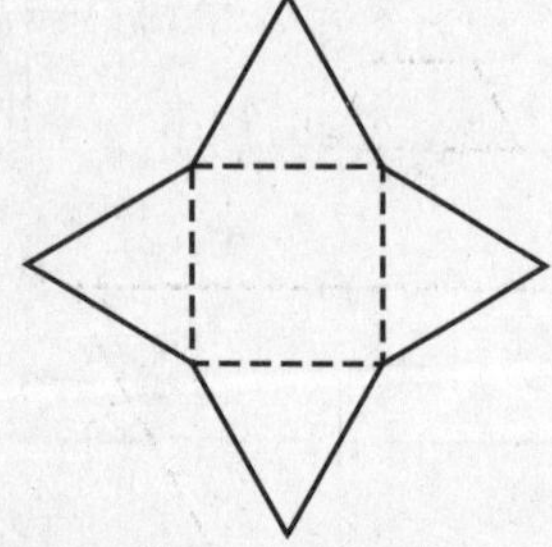

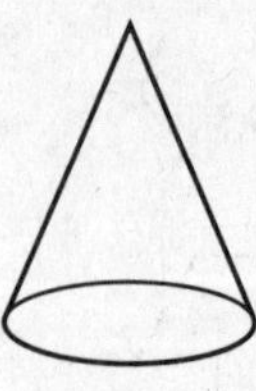

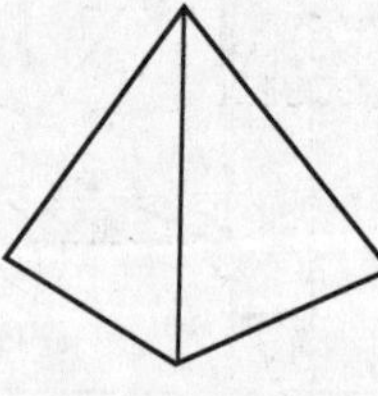

It has 4 triangular faces
and 1 square face.

2.

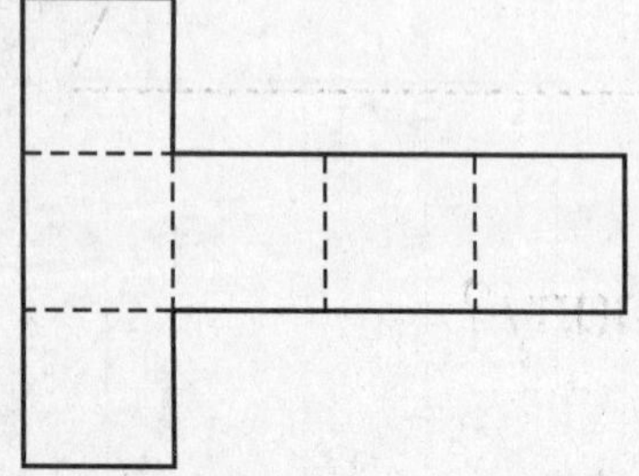

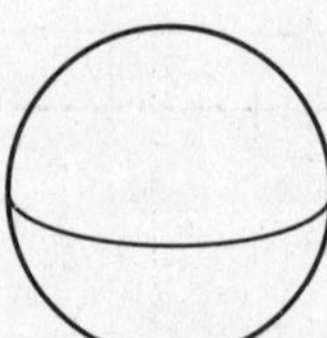

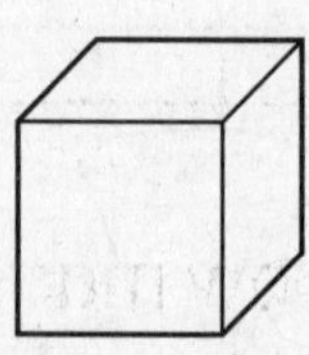

It has 6 square faces.

Name ________________________________

Making New Shapes

R 7-4

You can make a larger shape from smaller shapes.
Use pattern blocks.

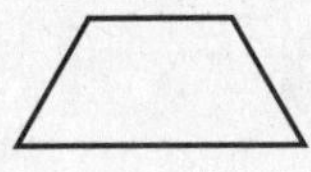

trapezoid

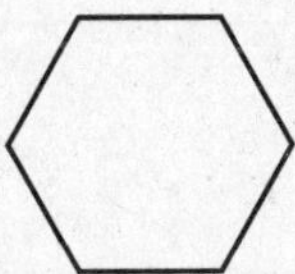

hexagon

2 trapezoids make 1 hexagon.

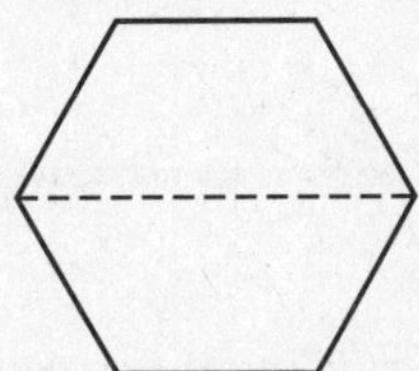

The larger shape has
 sides and 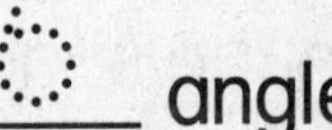 angles.

Use the pattern blocks shown to make the larger shapes.
Trace the shapes to show all the sides.

1.

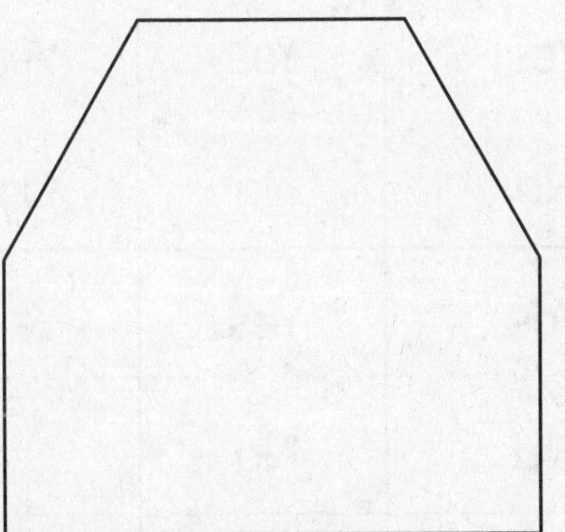

How many?

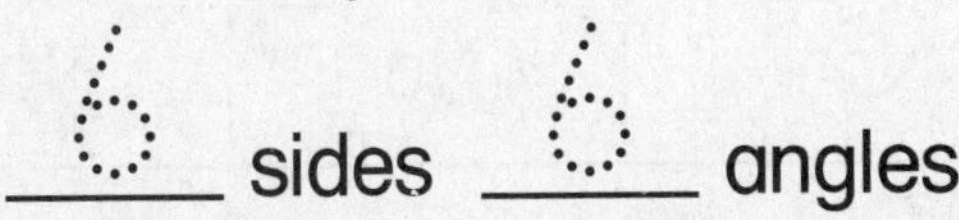

______ sides ______ angles

2.

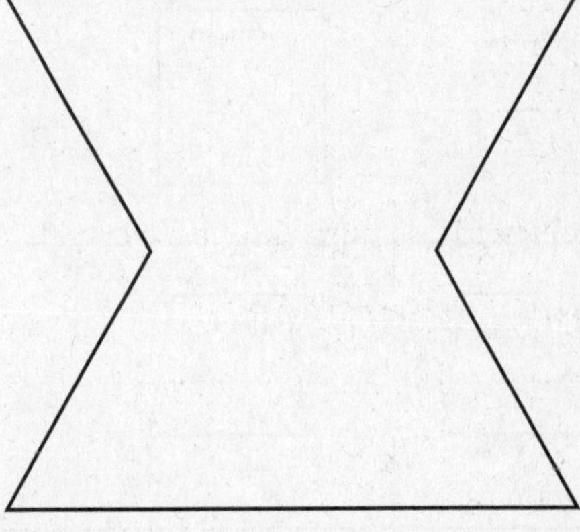

How many?

______ sides ______ angles

Name ______________________________

Congruence

R 7-5

These rectangles are not the same shape.

They are not congruent.

These rectangles are not the same size.

They are not congruent.

These rectangles are the same shape and same size.

They are congruent.

Are the shapes congruent? Circle **Yes** or **No.**

	Same Shape	Same Size	Congruent
1.	Yes No	Yes No	Yes No
2.	Yes No	Yes No	Yes No
3.	Yes No	Yes No	Yes No
4.	Yes No	Yes No	Yes No

Name ____________________

Slides, Flips, and Turns

R 7-6

You can slide shapes.	You can flip shapes.	You can turn shapes.
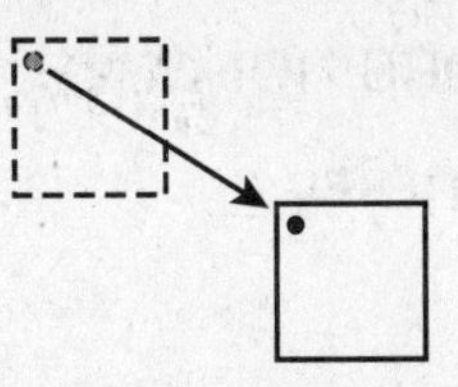	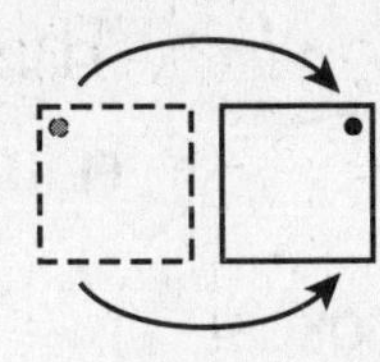	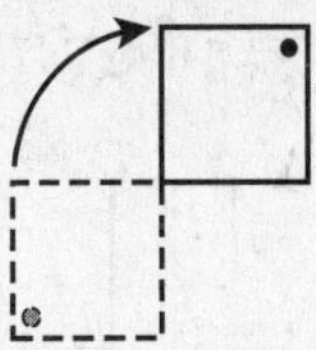

1. Circle the shape that slides.

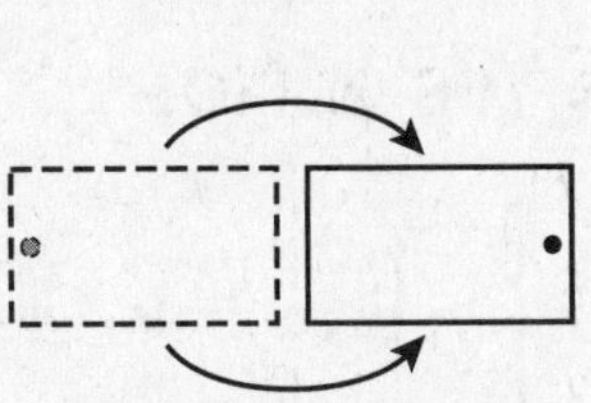

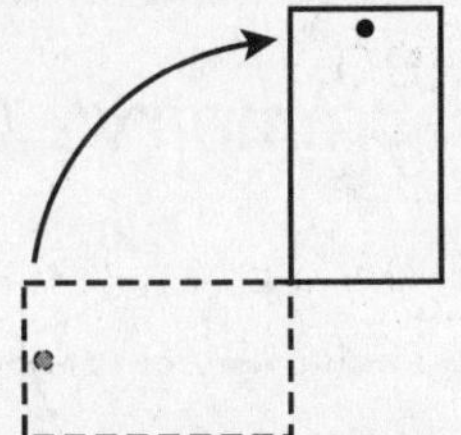

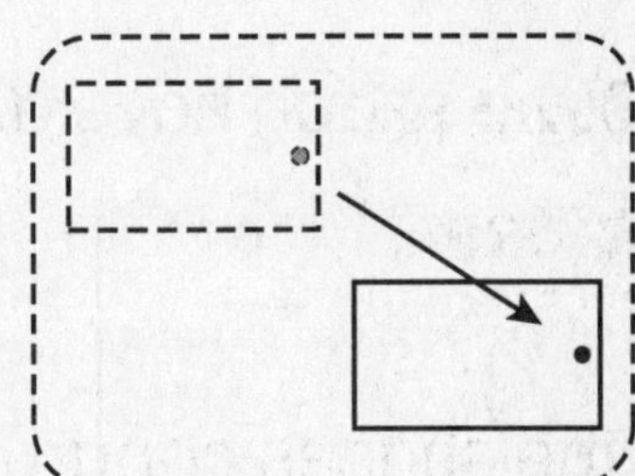

2. Circle the shape that flips.

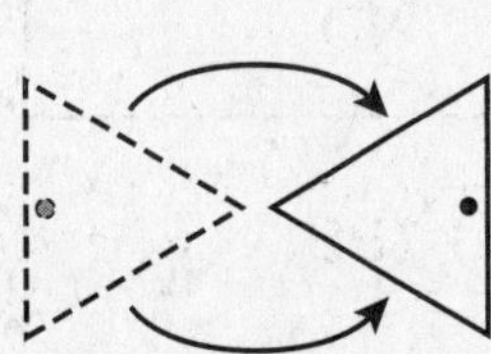

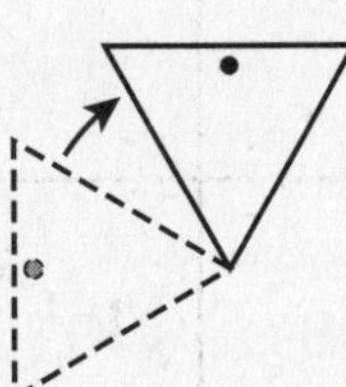

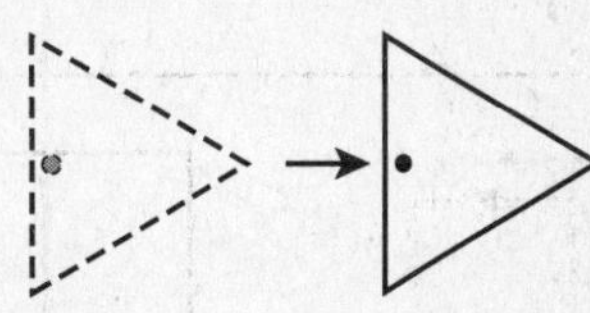

3. Circle the shape that turns.

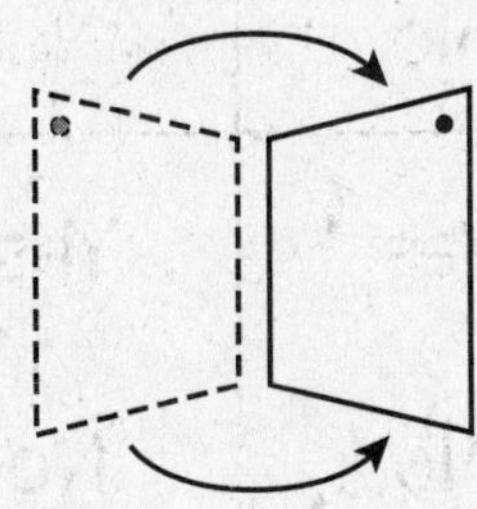

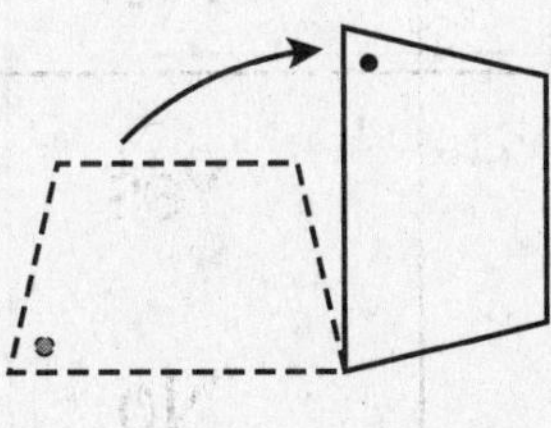

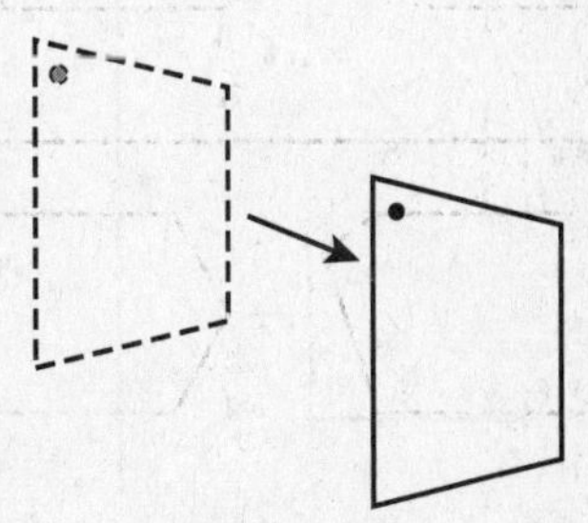

Name ________________________________

Symmetry

Both parts match. This shape has a line of symmetry.

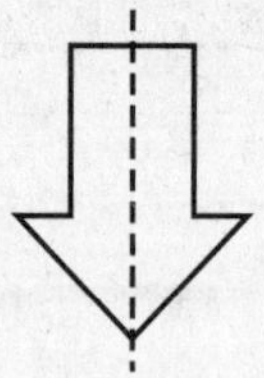

A line of symmetry makes 2 matching parts.

The parts do not match. This shape does not have a line of symmetry.

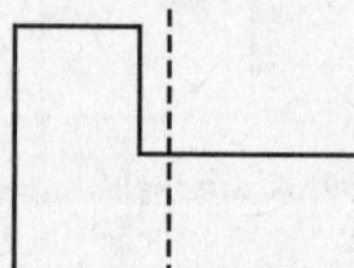

Does the shape have a line of symmetry? Circle **Yes** or **No.**

1.

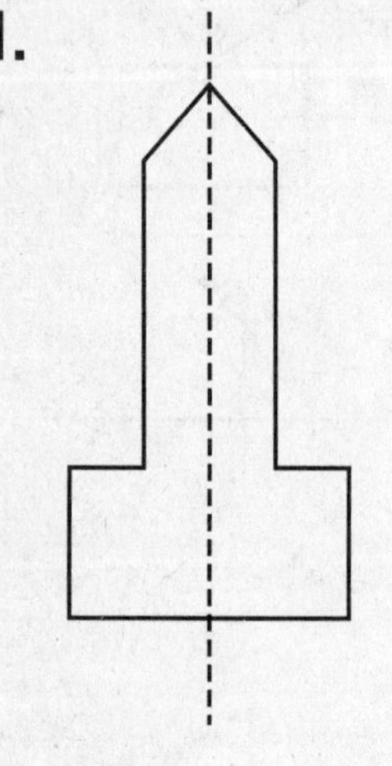

Yes No

2.

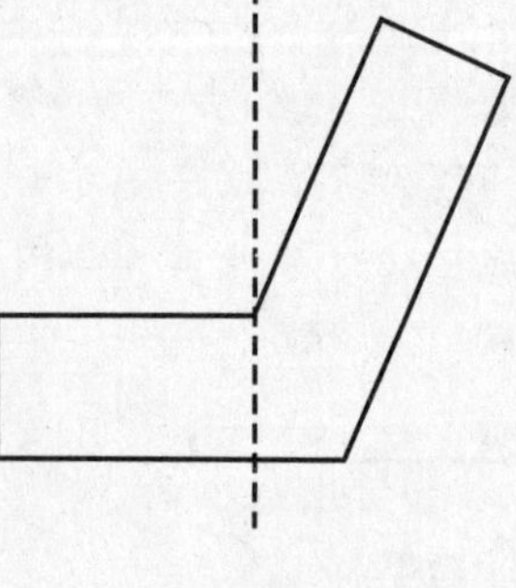

Yes No

3.

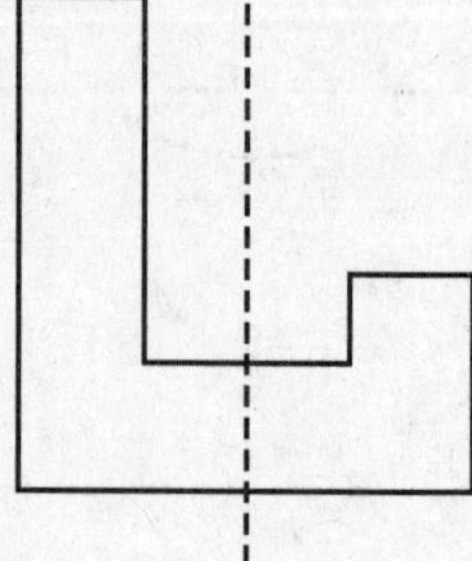

Yes No

Draw the line of symmetry for each shape.

4.

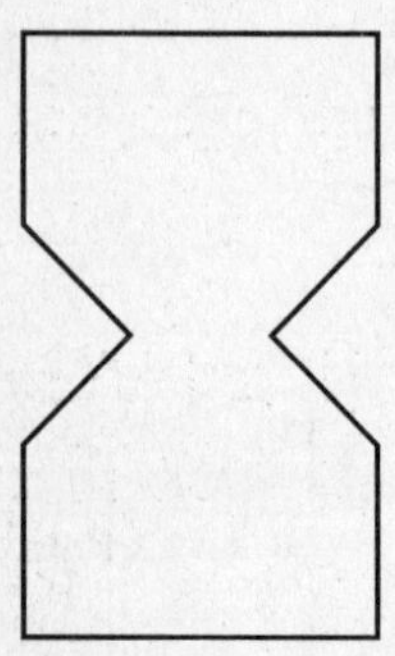

5.

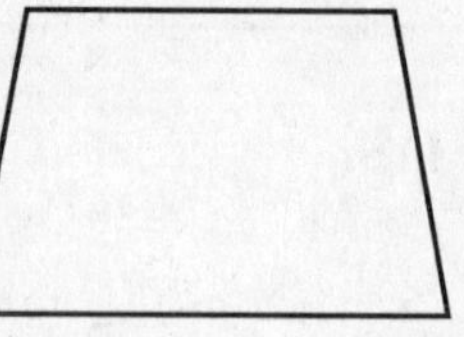

6.

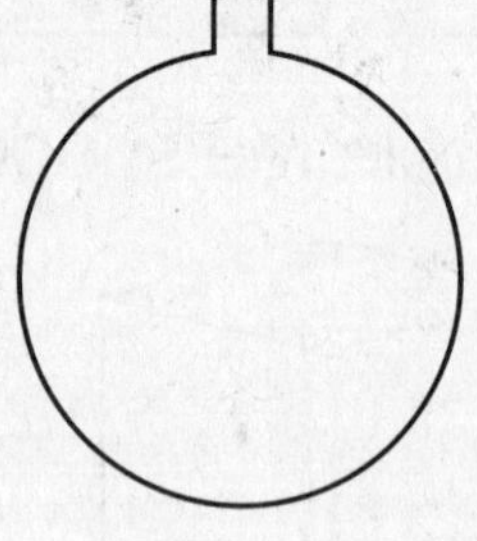

Name ____________________

PROBLEM-SOLVING STRATEGY **R 7-8**

Use Logical Reasoning

I am not a square.
I do not have 4 sides.
Which shape am I?

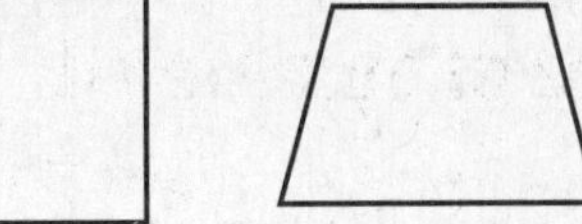

Read and Understand

Find the shape that answers the question.

Plan and Solve

Cross out the shapes that do not fit the clues.

1st Clue: I am not a square. So, cross out the square.

Which shape is not crossed out?

2nd Clue: I do not have 4 sides. So, cross out any shape with 4 sides.

Look Back and Check

Does your answer match the clues?

Cross out the shapes that do not fit the clues.
Circle the shape that is left. Answer the questions.

1. I do not have 5 angles.
   I am not a rectangle.
   Which shape am I?

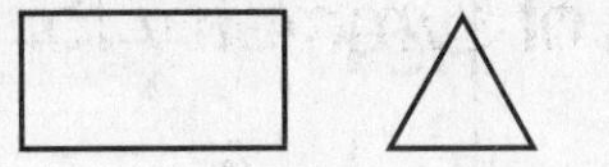

How many angles do I have?

______________________ ____

2. I do not have 6 sides.
   I am not a circle.
   Which shape am I?

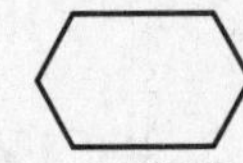

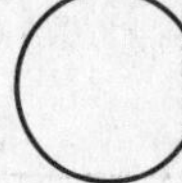

How many angles do I have?

______________________ ____

Name ____________________

Equal Parts

R 7-9

Equal parts are the same shape and size.

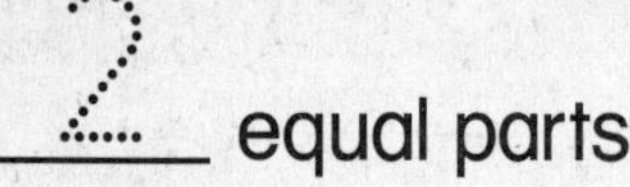

equal parts

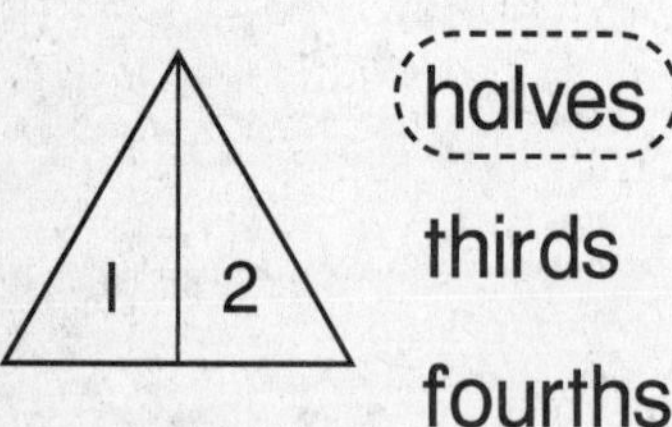

halves (circled)
thirds
fourths

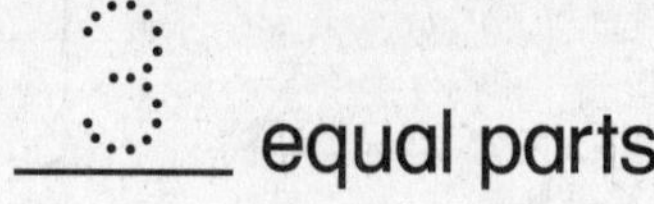

equal parts

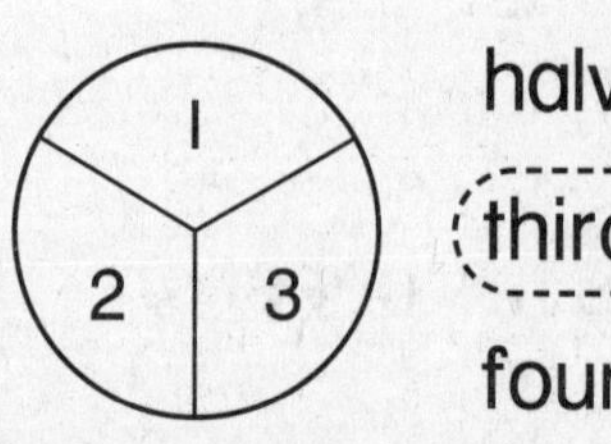

halves
thirds (circled)
fourths

4 equal parts

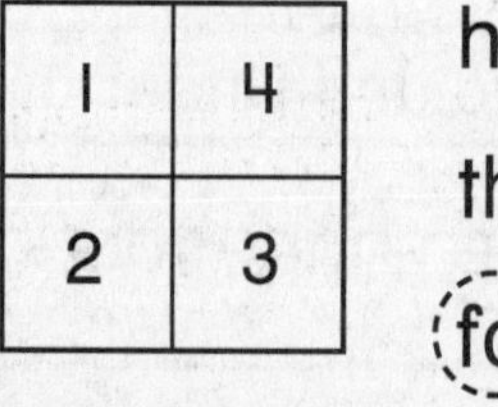

halves
thirds
fourths (circled)

How many equal parts? Write the number of parts and circle halves, thirds, or fourths.

1. _____ equal parts

halves
thirds
fourths

2. _____ equal parts

halves
thirds
fourths

3. _____ equal parts

halves
thirds
fourths

4. _____ equal parts

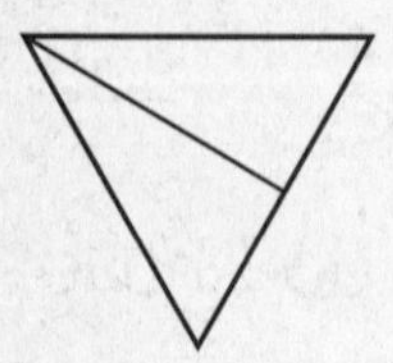

halves
thirds
fourths

5. _____ equal parts

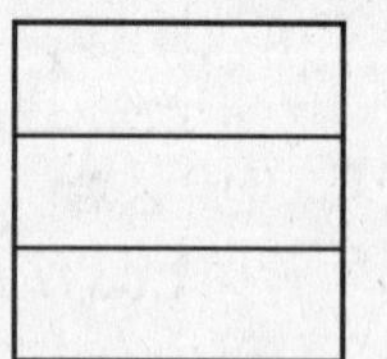

halves
thirds
fourths

6. _____ equal parts

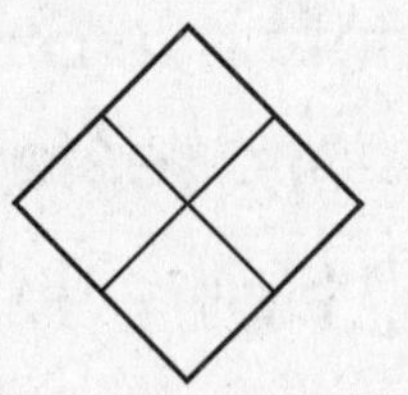

halves
thirds
fourths

Problem Solving *Visual Thinking*

Draw lines to show 2 equal parts.

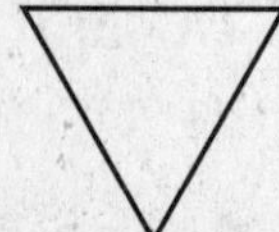
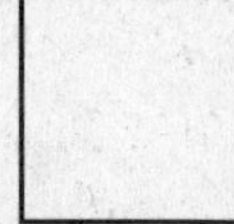
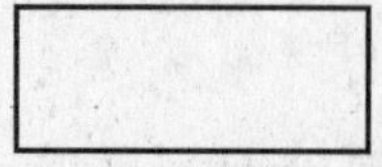

Name ______________________________

Estimating Fractions

R 7-12

To estimate fractions, think about the number of equal parts in the whole.

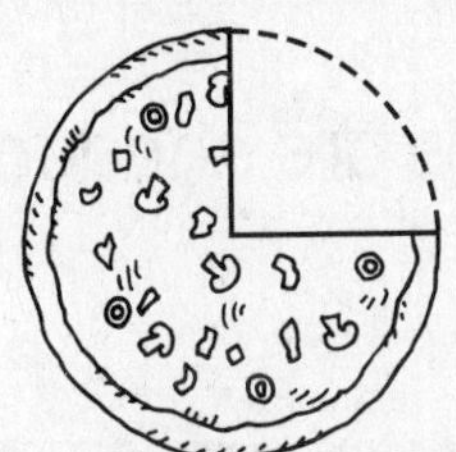

About $\frac{1}{4}$ of the pizza was eaten.

About $\frac{3}{4}$ of the pizza is left.

Think: There were about 4 equal pieces in this pizza.

About how much is left? Circle the best estimate.

1\.

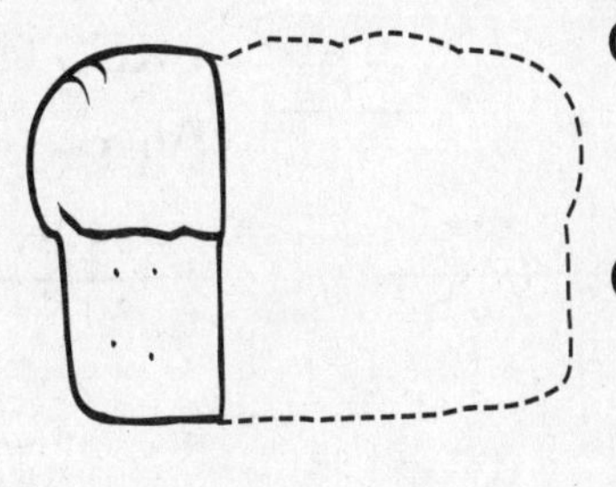

about $\frac{1}{3}$

about $\frac{1}{2}$

about $\frac{1}{4}$

2\.

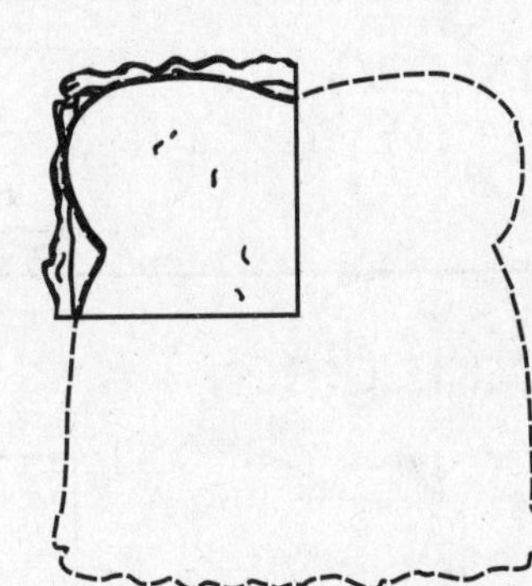

about $\frac{1}{2}$

about $\frac{1}{4}$

about $\frac{3}{4}$

3\.

about $\frac{2}{3}$

about $\frac{1}{2}$

about $\frac{3}{4}$

4\.

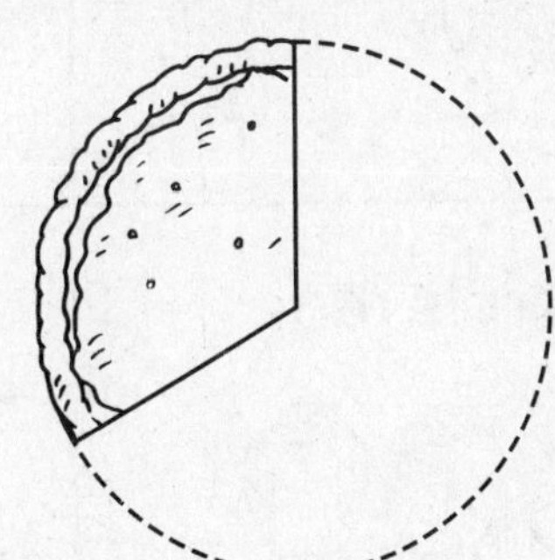

about $\frac{1}{2}$

about $\frac{2}{3}$

about $\frac{1}{3}$

Name ______________________________

Fractions of a Set

R 7-13

A fraction can name the equal parts of a set or a group.

2 shaded balls

5 balls in all

of the balls are shaded.

Color the parts.
Write the fraction for the part you color.

1. Color 2 parts blue.

blue stars

stars in all

of the stars are blue.

2. Color 3 parts green.

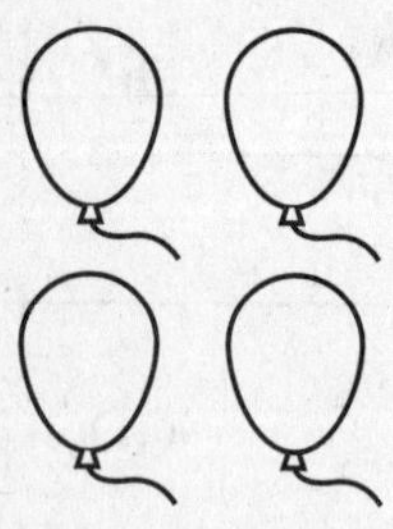

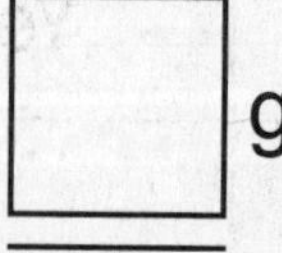

green balloons

balloons in all

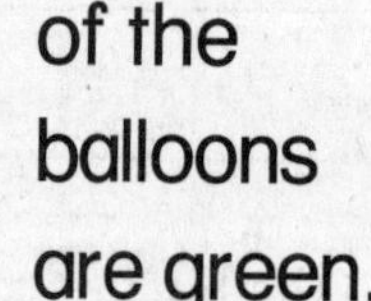

of the balloons are green.

3. Color 5 parts red.

red apples

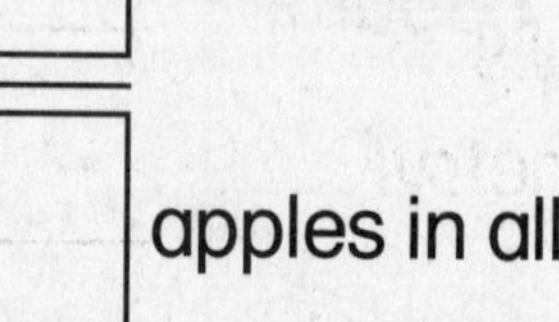

apples in all

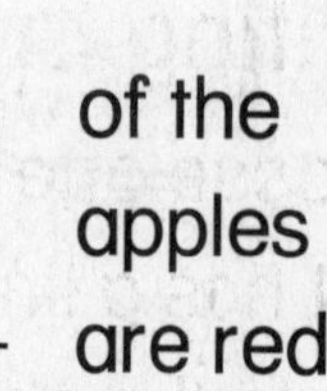

of the apples are red.

Name ____________________

PROBLEM SOLVING APPLICATIONS **R 7-14**

Under the Sea

Some shells have a line of symmetry.
Some shells do not have a line of symmetry.

This shell does not have a line of symmetry.

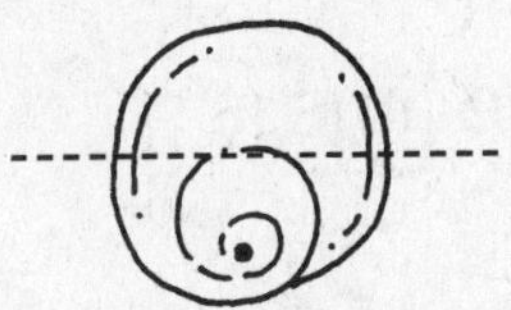

Both parts do not match.

This shell has a line of symmetry.

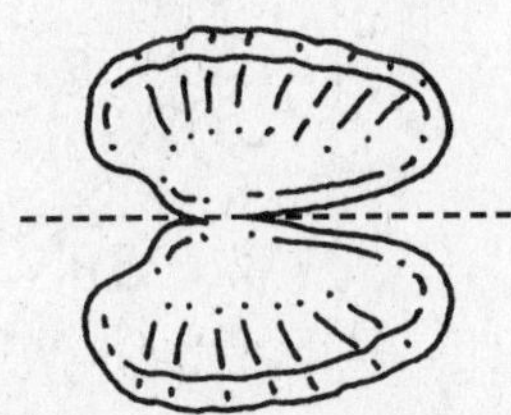

Both parts match.

Does the shell have a line of symmetry?
Circle **Yes** or **No.**

1.

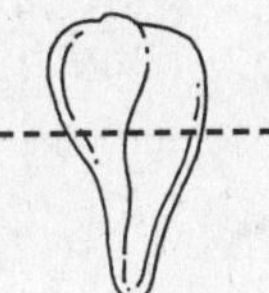

Yes No

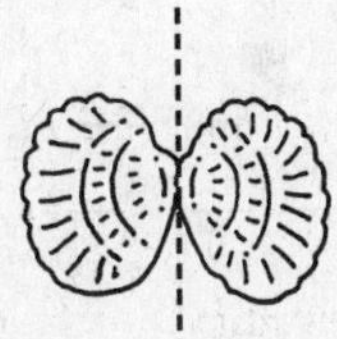

Yes No

2.

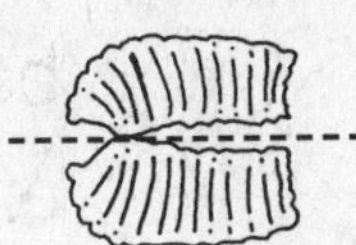

Yes No

Yes No

Writing in Math

Choose one of the shells that has a line of symmetry.
Circle the shell.
Write a sentence to describe the shell.

____

____

____

Name ______________________________

Telling Time to Five Minutes

R 8-1

It takes five minutes for the minute hand to move from number to number.

To tell time to five minutes count by 5s for every number.

The time is 5:15

Count by 5s. Write the time.

1.

2.

3.

4.

Problem Solving *Reasoning*

5. The time is 6:10. Is the hour hand closer to 6 or 7? Why?

____

____

Name ________________________________

Telling Time After the Hour

R 8-2

There are different ways to say time after the hour.

15 minutes after 6
or
quarter past 6

30 minutes after 6
or
half past 6

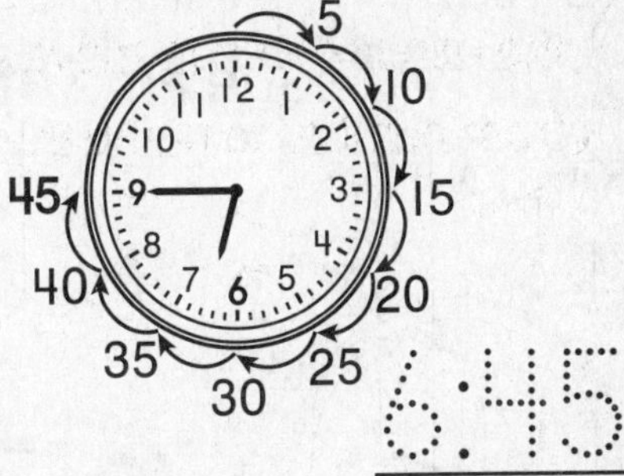

45 minutes after 6

Count by fives to tell the time. Write the time.

1. 

30 minutes after 3
or half past 3

2. 

___ : ___

15 minutes after 8
or quarter past 8

3. 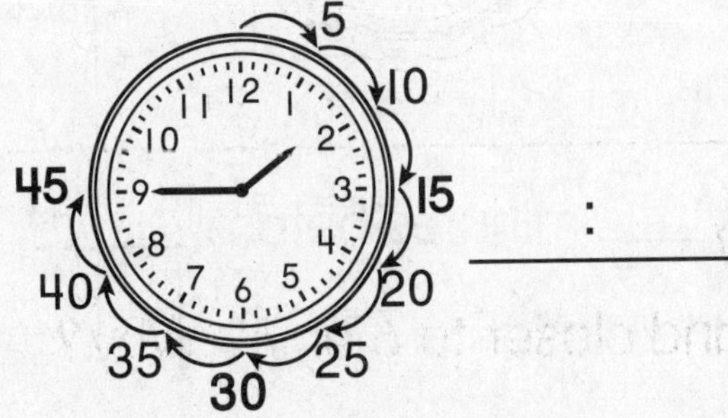

___ : ___

45 minutes after 1

4. 

___ : ___

45 minutes after 5

Name ______________________________

Telling Time Before the Hour

R 8-3

Count by 5s from the 12 to the minute hand to say or write the time **after** the hour.

Count by 5s from the minute hand to the 12 to say or write the time **before** the hour.

35 minutes **after** 2 is the same as 25 minutes **before** 3

Write the time or draw the minute hand to show the time.
Write the time before the hour.

1.

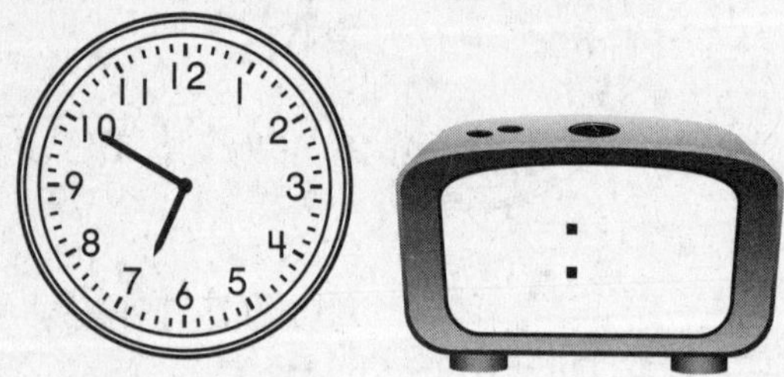

_____ minutes before _____

2.

_____ minutes before _____

Name ________________________________

Estimating Time

R 8-4

About how long does it take to wash your face?

about 1 minute (circled) — Is 1 minute reasonable? Yes.

about 1 hour — Is 1 hour reasonable? No, it's too long.

about 1 day — Is 1 day reasonable? No, it's too long.

Circle the amount of time each activity will take.

1. Drinking milk

about 1 minute

about 1 hour

about 1 day

2. Watching a TV show

about 1 minute

about 1 hour

about 1 day

3. Going on a picnic

about 2 minutes

about 2 hours

about 2 days

4. Going on a trip

about 5 minutes

about 5 hours

about 5 days

Name ______________________

Elapsed Time

R 8-5

Count the number of hours to find out how much time has passed.

Count from the start time to the end time.

Starts	Ends	Starts	Ends

3:00	5:00	7:00	10:00
(2 hours)	3 hours	2 hours	(3 hours)

Write the times. Then circle how many hours have passed.

1.

Starts	Ends
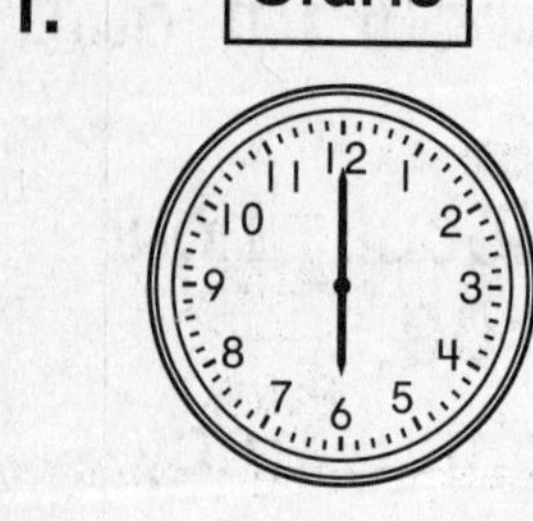	
______	______
1 hour	2 hours

2.

Starts	Ends

______	______
7 hours	3 hours

3.

Starts	Ends

______	______
3 hours	4 hours

4.

Starts	Ends

______	______
5 hours	6 hours

Name ______________________________

A.M. and P.M.

R 8-6

There are two 12:00s in one day.

12:00 A.M.

Most of us are asleep.

12:00 P.M.

Most of us are eating lunch.

A.M. starts at 12:00 midnight. It ends at noon.

P.M. starts at 12:00 noon. It ends at midnight.

Is it A.M. or P.M.?

3:00 A.M. P.M.

8:00 A.M. P.M.

9:00 A.M. P.M.

Circle A.M. or P.M. to tell the time.

1. 8:00 A.M. P.M.

2. 7:00 A.M. P.M.

3. 10:00 A.M. P.M.

Name ____________________

Using a Calendar

R 8-7

There are 12 months in one year.
March is the 3rd month of the year.

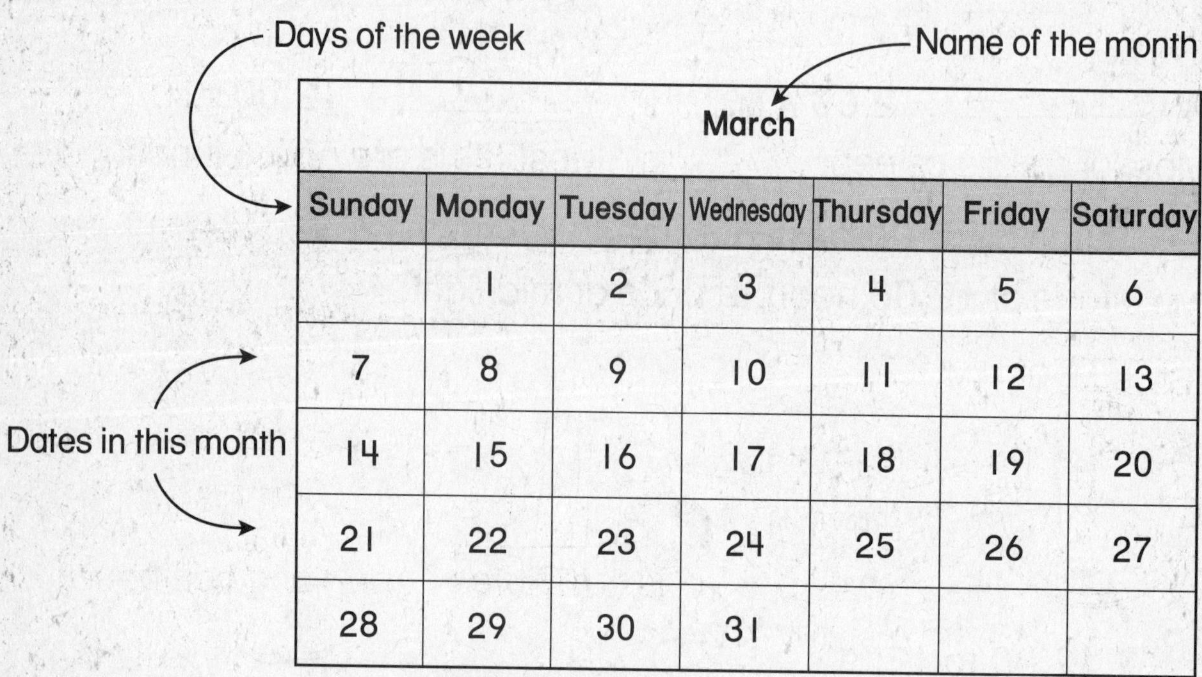

March

Sunday	Monday	Tuesday	Wednesday	Thursday	Friday	Saturday
	1	2	3	4	5	6
7	8	9	10	11	12	13
14	15	16	17	18	19	20
21	22	23	24	25	26	27
28	29	30	31			

Look at the last date in the month to find how many days in March.

Use the calendar to answer the questions.

1. What day is the first day of March? ____________________

2. What day is the 16th? ____________________

3. What is the day after Wednesday? ____________________

4. What is the date of the third Friday? ______________

5. How many days are in March altogether? ______________

Name ______________________________

Equivalent Times

R 8-8

Equivalent time is another way to say the same time.

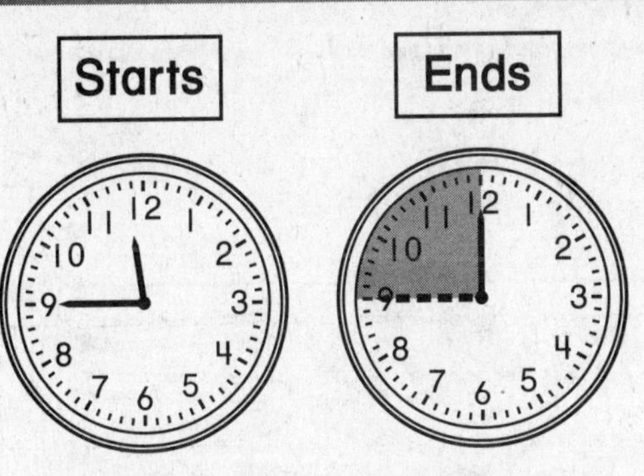

11:45 to 12:00

is 15 minutes or one quarter hour

12:00 to 12:30

is 30 minutes or one half hour

12:30 to 1:30

is 60 minutes or one hour

Circle the equivalent time.

1. Mario reads from 12:00 to 12:30.

   30 minutes　　60 minutes　　15 minutes

2. Jamal sings for 15 minutes.

   one quarter hour　　one half hour　　one hour

Name ______________________________

PROBLEM-SOLVING STRATEGY **R 8-9**

Make a Table

Sasha had a box of school supplies.
How many of each kind of school supply are there?

Read and Understand

What are the supplies?
How many of each are there?

Plan and Solve

Think: What do I need to find out?

Complete the table. Count the objects.
Use one tally mark for each object.

Look Back and Check

How does the table help you organize information?

____

____

____

School Supplies	
Kinds	Number
Crayons	| |
Tape	|
Pencils	
Erasers	

Now use the table to answer the questions.

1. How many crayons are there? 2
2. How many pencils are there? _____
3. Are there more crayons or pencils? ______________
4. How many more erasers are there than pencils? _____

Name ____

Recording Data from a Survey

R 8-10

Take a **survey** to collect information. Information is called **data.** Make tally marks to record this **data.**

Favorite Frozen Yogurt Flavors

Vanilla	Chocolate	Strawberry
𝍸𝍷	𝍸𝍷𝍷	𝍷𝍷𝍷𝍷

Use the survey to answer the questions.

1. Which flavor is the favorite of the greatest number of children?

   ____

2. Which flavor did the least number of children choose?

   ____

3. How many children in all answered the survey? ____

4. How many more children chose vanilla than strawberry? ____

Name ______________________________

Using a Venn Diagram

R 8-11

A Venn diagram can be used to collect and show information. It can show how many people like different things and how many people like both things.

Do you like hot dogs, hamburgers, or both?

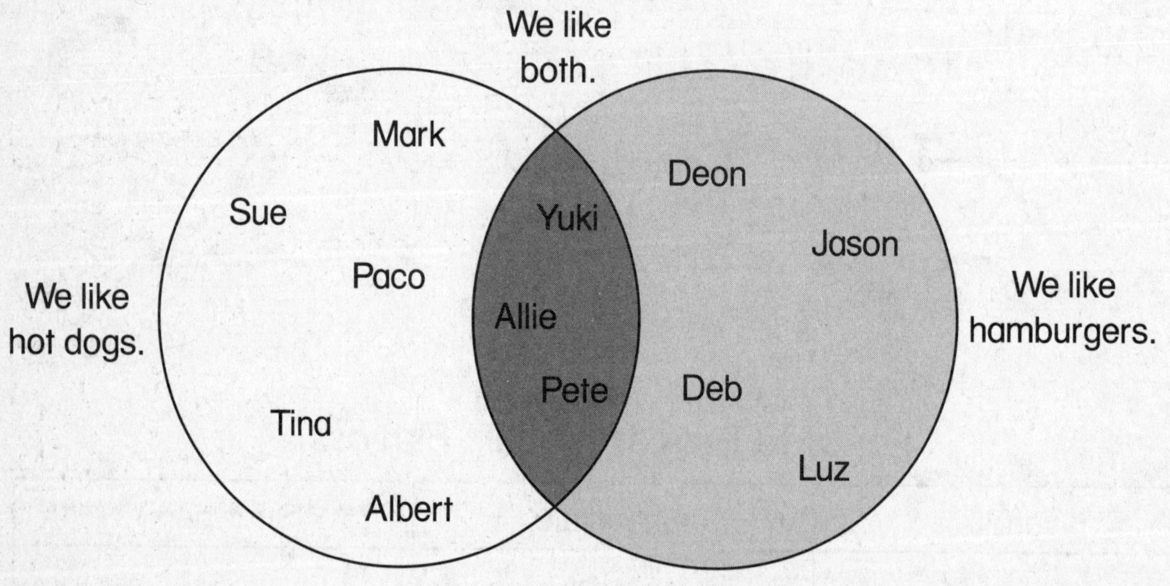

Use the diagram to answer the questions.

1. Draw a line under the names of children who like only hot dogs.

2. Circle the names of children who like only hamburgers.

3. Draw an X over the names of children who like both hot dogs and hamburgers.

4. How many children like hamburgers? _____ children

5. How many children were surveyed altogether? _____ children

Name ______________________________

Pictographs

R 8-12

A pictograph uses pictures or symbols to show information.

Write how many children chose each snack.

Each ☺ = 1 child

There are 9 symbols for popcorn. So 9 children chose popcorn.

Favorite Snacks

Popcorn	☺☺☺☺☺☺☺☺☺	9
Fruit Cups	☺☺☺☺	____
Yogurt	☺☺☺☺☺☺☺	____
Cheese and Crackers	☺☺☺☺☺☺☺☺☺☺	____

Use the graph to answer the questions.

1. How many children like cheese and crackers the best? ____ children

2. How many children like yogurt the best? ____ children

3. Which snack is the least favorite? ____________

4. Which snack is favored by most children? ____________

5. How many more children like yogurt than fruit cups? ____ children

6. How many more children like cheese and crackers than yogurt ? ____ children

Name ______________________________

Bar Graphs

R 8-13

A bar graph uses bars to show information.
The name of the graph tells the kind of information.

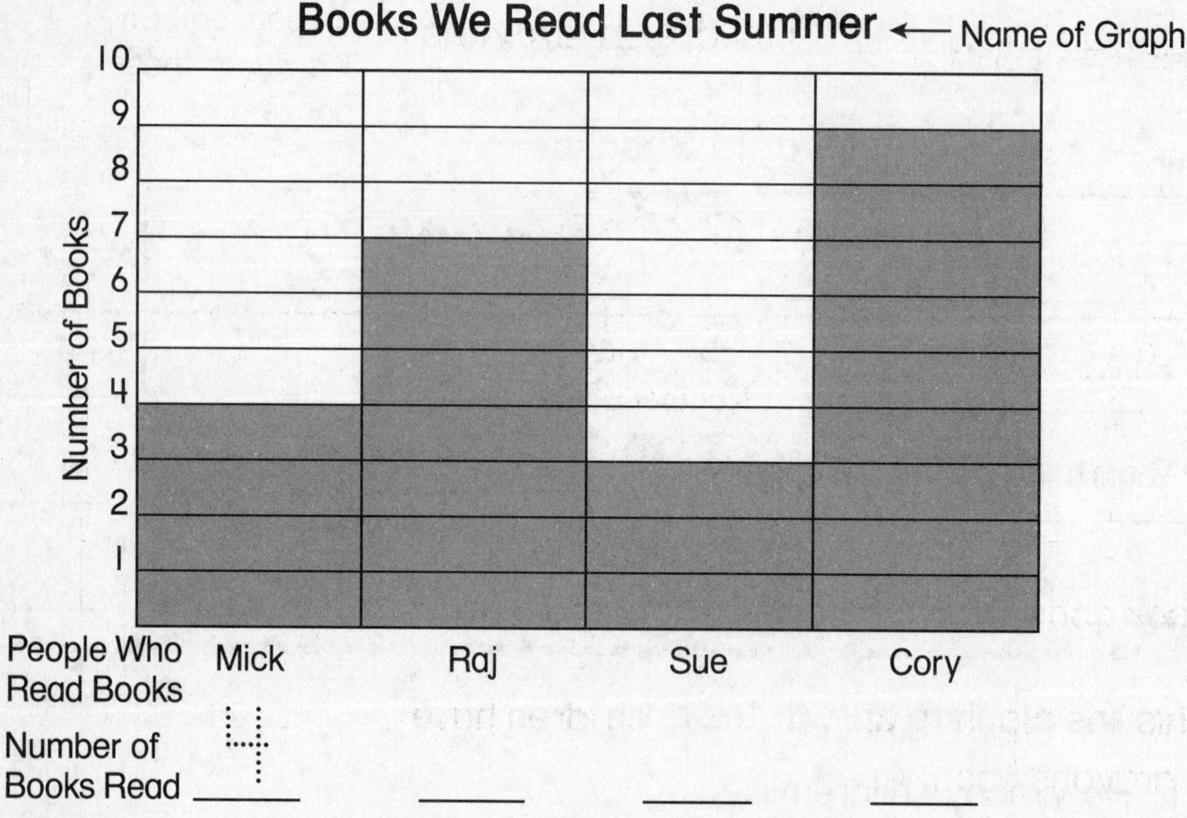

Count the number of colored boxes and write the number.
These numbers tell how many books each person read.

Use the graph to answer the questions.

1. How many books did Mick read last summer? __4__ books

2. How many books did Sue and Raj read last summer? ______ books

3. Who read the most books? ____________

4. Who read the least books? ____________

Name ____________________

Line Plots

R 8-14

A line plot is another way to show how many.
Look at the parts of the line plot.

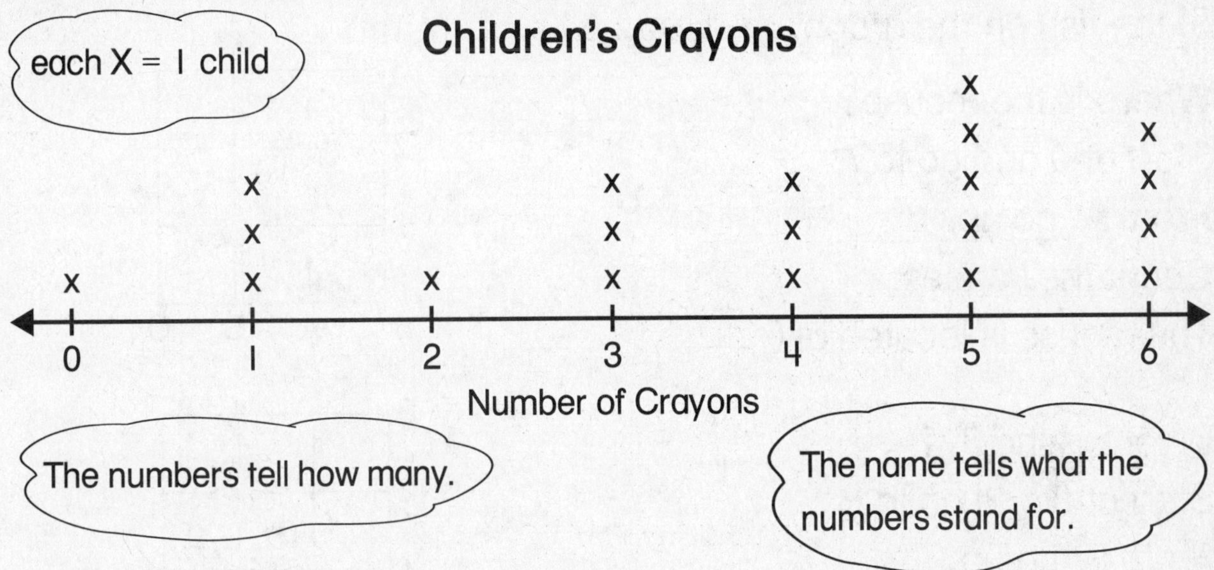

Look above the number 4. There are 3 Xs.

This line plot shows that __3__ children have 4 crayons each.

Look above the number 6. There are 4 Xs. This line plot shows that __4__ children have 6 crayons each.

Use the line plot to answer the questions.

1. How many children have 3 crayons? _____ children
2. How many children have 1 crayon? _____ children
3. How many children have 0 crayons? _____ child
4. How many crayons did the most number of children have? _____ crayons

Name ________________________________

Coordinate Graphs

R 8-15

Coordinate graphs show where things are located.

The ordered pair (B, 1) names the location of the fish on the graph.

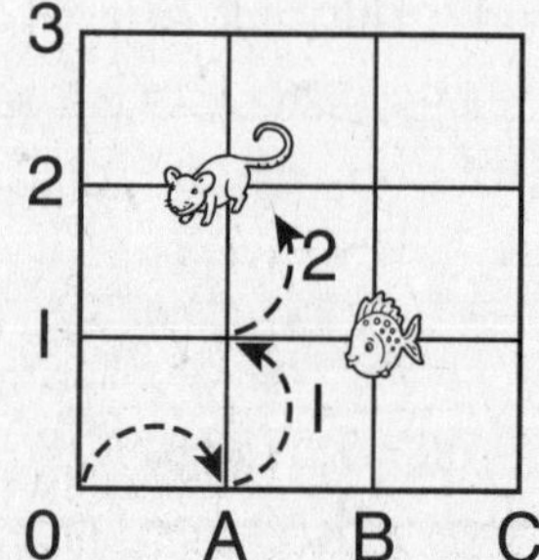

Where is the mouse?
Start at 0 and go to A.
From A, go up.
Count the spaces.
The mouse is located at (A, 2).

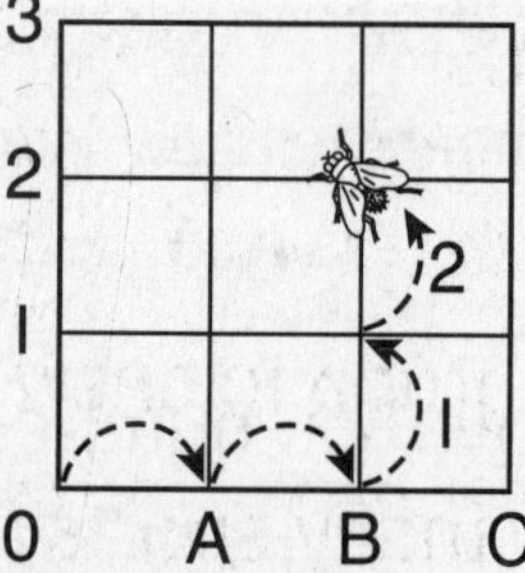

Where is the fly?
Start at 0 and go to B.
From B, go up.
Count the spaces.
The fly is located at (B, 2).

Write the ordered pair where each animal is located.

1. (A, ____)

2. (____, 1)

3. (____, ____)

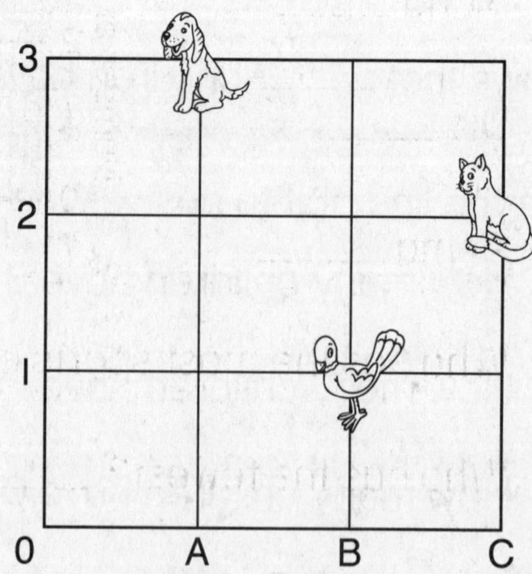

Name ____________________

PROBLEM-SOLVING SKILL **R 8-16**

Use Data from a Graph

A graph shows us information.

How many animals are there?

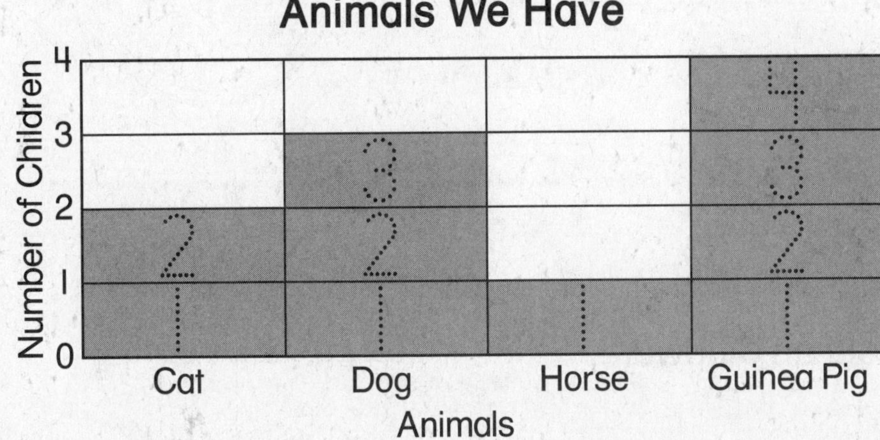

Cat 2

Dog 3

Horse 1

Guinea Pig 4

Use the graph to answer the questions.

1. How many sports cards does each child have?

John ______

Maria ______

Dia ______

Ahmad ______

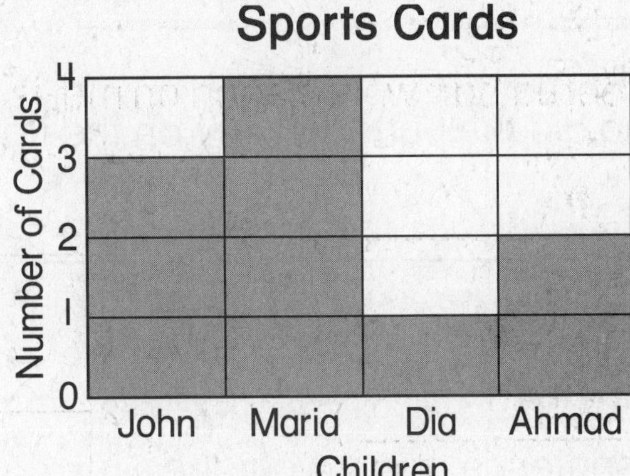

2. Who has the most sports cards? __________

3. Who has the fewest? __________

Name ______________________________

PROBLEM-SOLVING APPLICATIONS **R 8-17**

Fly, Butterfly, Fly!

The short hand tells the hour 1:_____.

The long hand tells the minutes _____:30.

The time is 1:30.

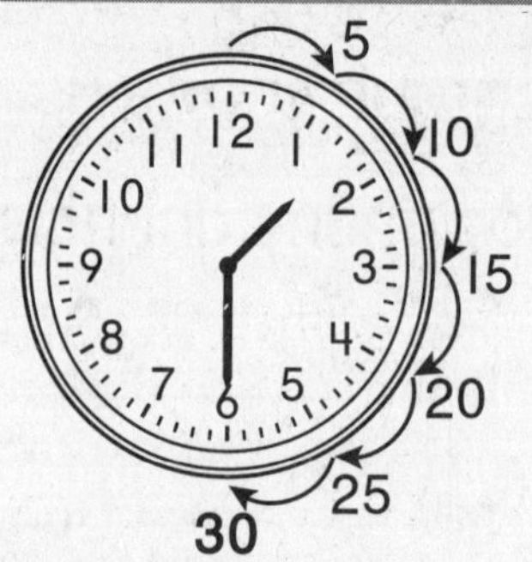

Write the time.

1. The butterfly rests on a flower.

____

2. The butterfly leaves the flower.

____

3. How long did the butterfly stay on the flower?

____

Writing in Math

4. Write a sentence about what the butterfly did next. Tell how long it took and show the time on the clock.

____

____

Name ________________

Understanding Length and Height

Height is how tall an object is.
You can use cubes to measure height.
Line up the cubes with the ends of the object.

about 2 cubes tall

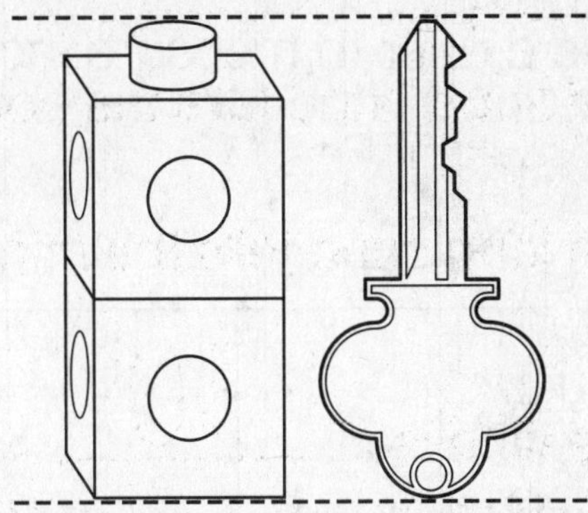

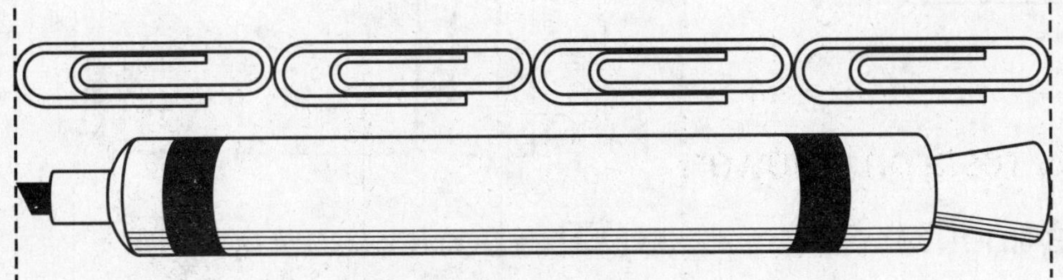

Length is how long an object is.
You can use paper clips to measure length. Line up the paper clips with the ends of the object.

about 4 paper clips long

1. Measure the height using cubes.

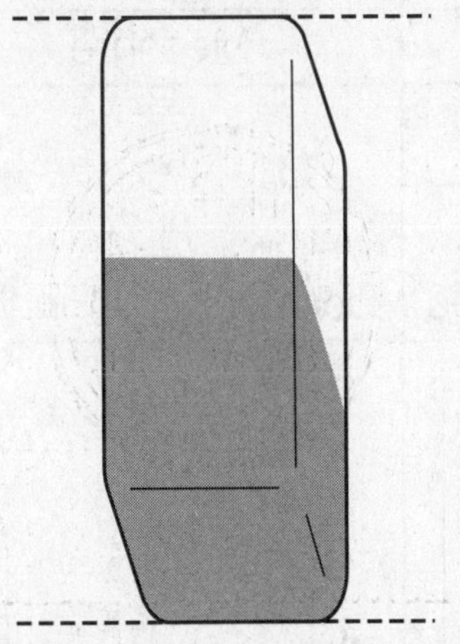

about _____ cubes tall

2. Measure the length using paper clips.

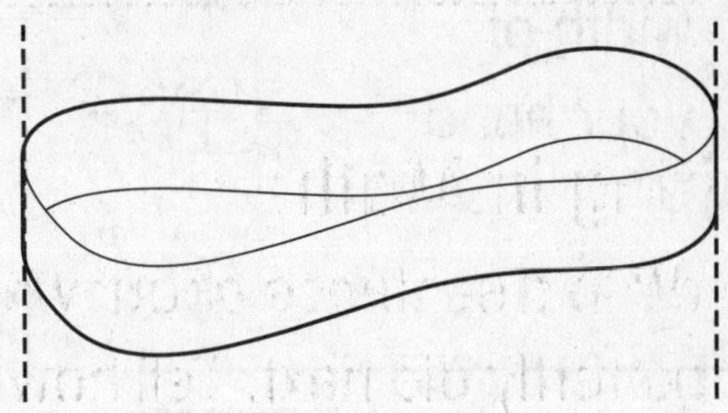

about _____ paper clips long

Name ____________________

Inches and Feet

R 9-2

Use a ruler to measure inches or feet.

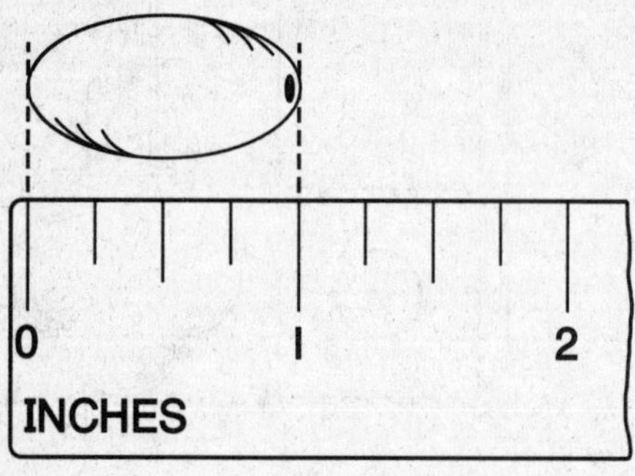

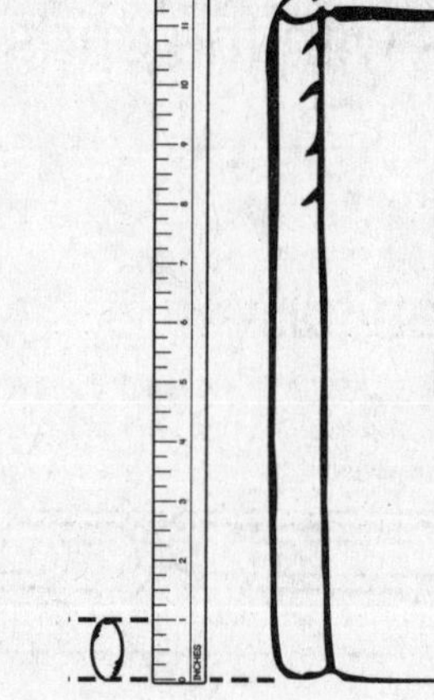

The bead is about

1 inch long.

The book is about

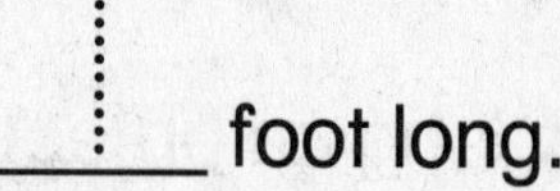

1 foot long.

There are 12 inches in 1 foot.

Estimate the width or height of each object.
Then use a ruler to measure.

		Estimate.	Measure.
1. width of your hand	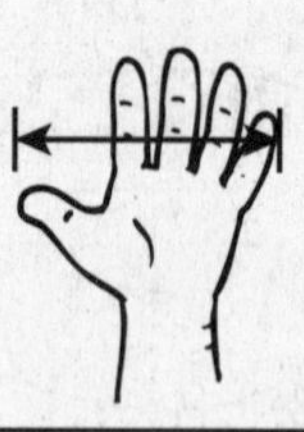	about ______ inches	about ______ inches
2. height of a door	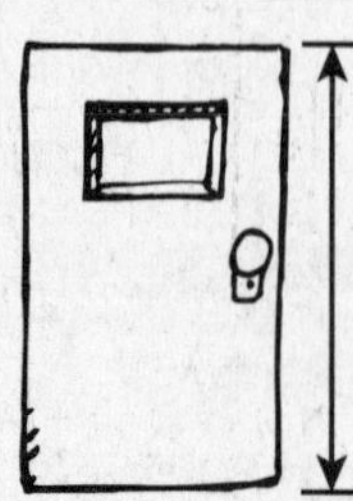	about ______ inches	about ______ inches

Name ______________________________

Inches, Feet, and Yards

R 9-3

Use inches to measure short lengths.
Use feet to measure medium-sized lengths.
Use **yards** to measure long lengths.

Remember:
3 feet = 1 yard
36 inches = 1 yard

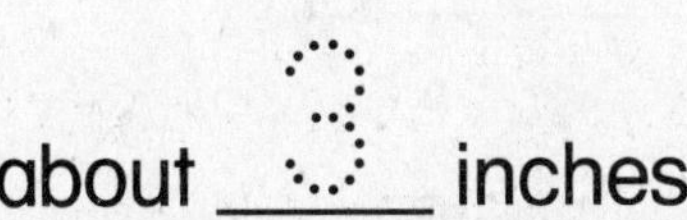

about 3 inches

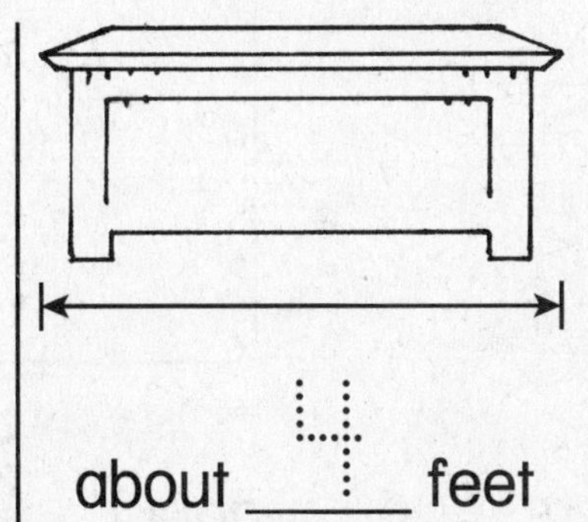

about 4 feet

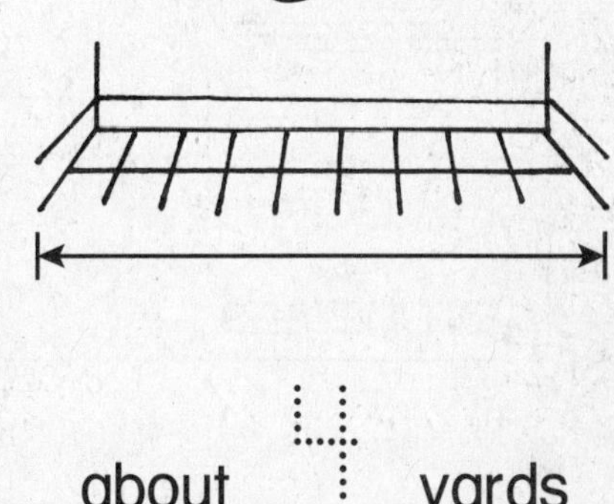

about 4 yards

Estimate. Then use a ruler to measure.

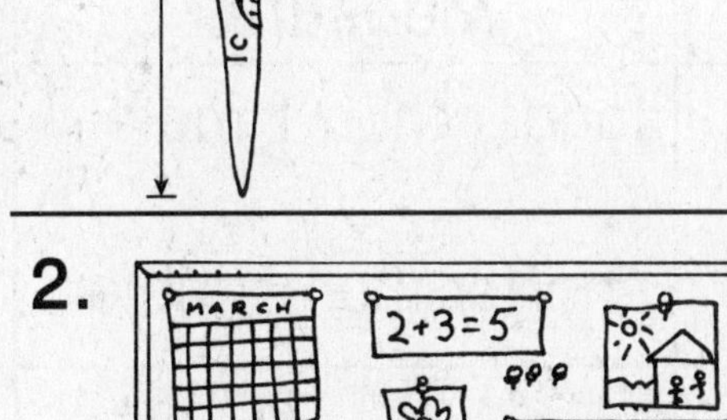

	Estimate.	Measure.
1.	about ______ inches	about ______ inches
2.	about ______ feet	about ______ feet

Estimate. Then use a yardstick to measure.

	Estimate.	Measure.
3.	about ______ yards	about ______ yards

Name ____________________

Centimeters and Meters

R 9-4

Centimeters are used to measure short lengths.
Meters are used to measure long lengths.

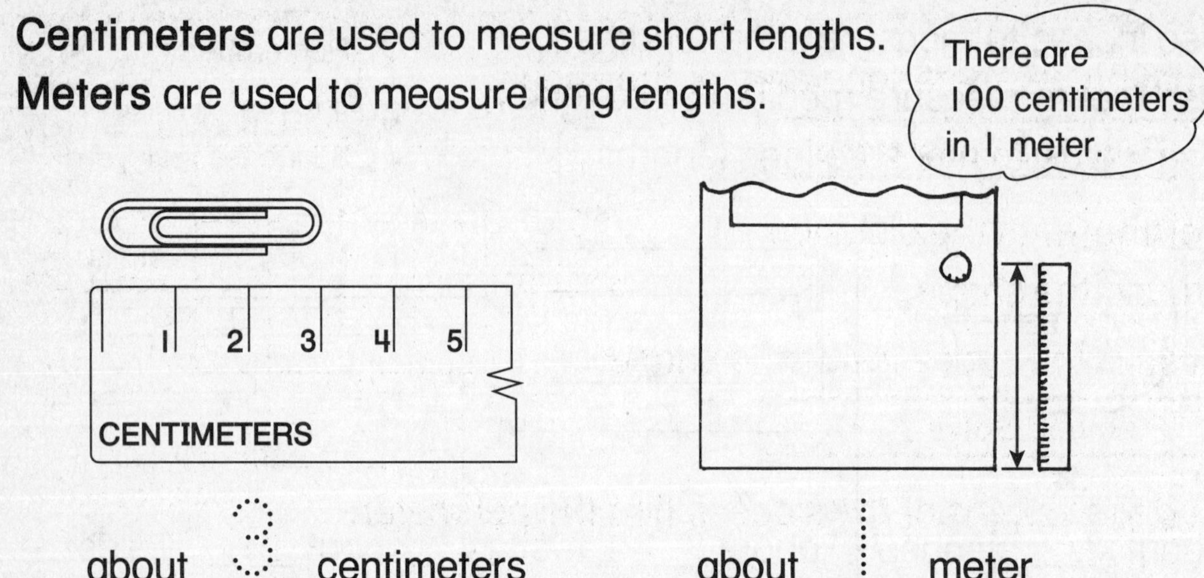

about __3__ centimeters   about __1__ meter

Estimate longer or shorter than 1 meter.
Then use a ruler to measure. Circle your answers.

	Estimate.	Measure.
1.	longer than 1 meter shorter than 1 meter	longer than 1 meter shorter than 1 meter
2.	longer than 1 meter shorter than 1 meter	longer than 1 meter shorter than 1 meter
3.	longer than 1 meter shorter than 1 meter	longer than 1 meter shorter than 1 meter

Name ____________________

PROBLEM-SOLVING STRATEGY **R 9-5**

Act It Out

Find the perimeter and area of the shape.

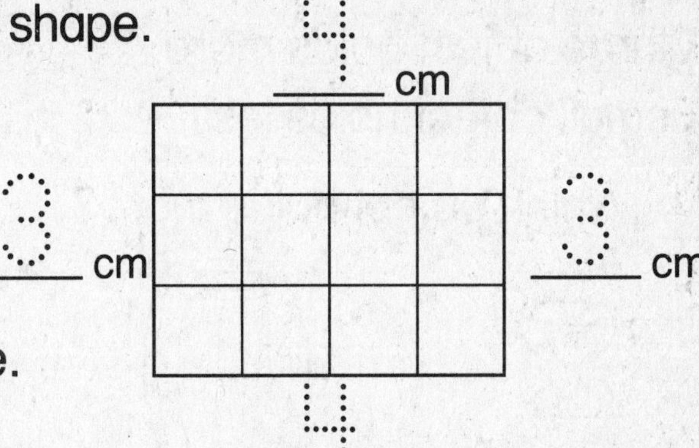

Read and Understand

Perimeter is the distance around the shape.

Area is the space inside the shape.

Plan and Solve

Add the lengths of the sides to find the perimeter.

4 cm + 3 cm + 4 cm + 3 cm = 14 cm

Count the square units inside the shape.

The area of the shape is 12 square units.

Look Back and Check

Did you add together all the sides? Did you count all the square units?

Find the perimeter and area of the shape.

I.

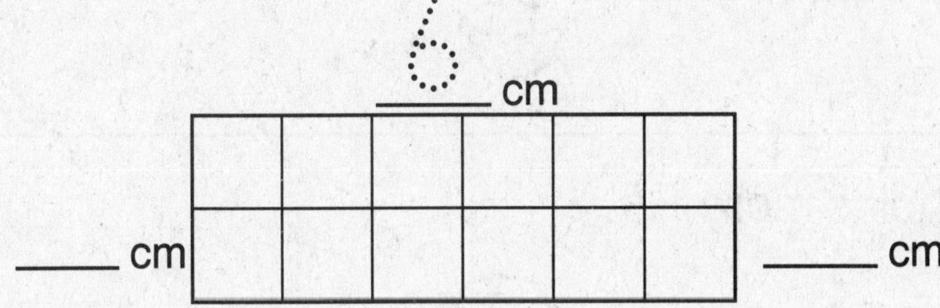

____ cm

____ cm + ____ cm + ____ cm + ____ cm = ____ cm

The perimeter is ____ cm.

The area is ____ square units.

Name ______________________________

Understanding Capacity

Capacity is the amount a container holds.
A large object holds more.
A small object holds less.

Which object holds more?

Which object holds less?

Circle the object that holds more.

1.

Circle the object that holds less.

2.

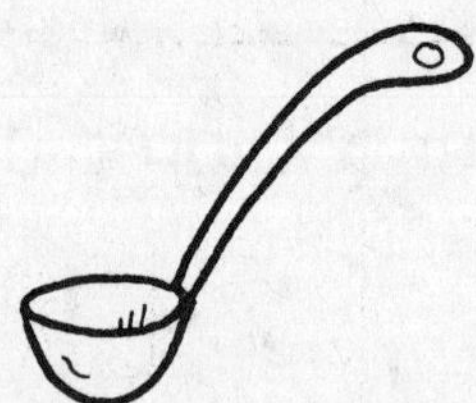

Circle the object that holds more.

3.

Name ______________________________

Cups, Pints, and Quarts

R 9-7

Use **cups, pints,** and **quarts** to measure capacity.

 I cup	 I pint	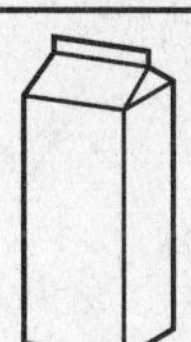 I quart
A cup holds less than a pint.	2 cups = I pint A pint holds less than a quart.	2 pints = I quart 4 cups = I quart

Circle the group on the right that shows the same amount.

I. 

I pint

2. 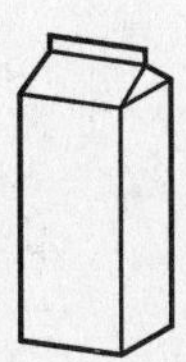

I quart

3. 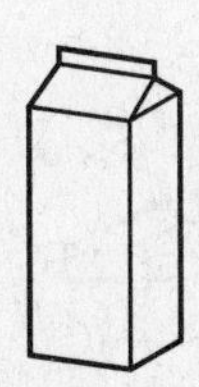

I quart

Name ______________________________

Liters

R 9-8

Liters are used to measure capacity.

This bottle of juice holds I liter.

This glass of juice holds

than I liter.

Circle the container that holds more than I liter.

I.

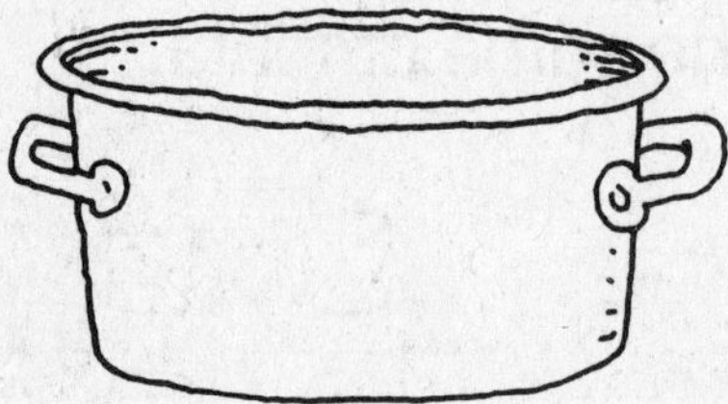

Circle the container that holds less than I liter.

2.

Circle the container that holds more than I liter.

3.

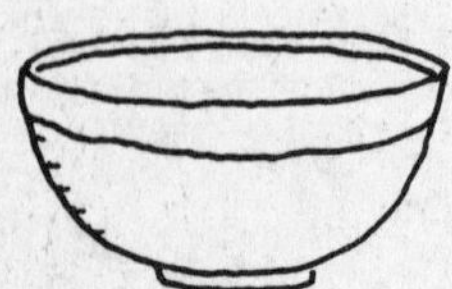

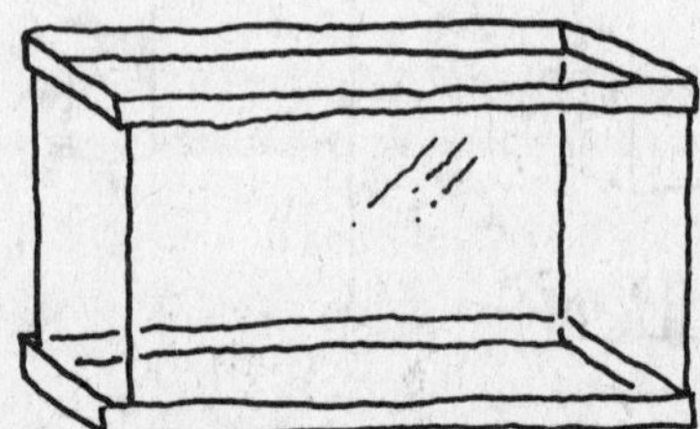

Name ____________________

Understanding Volume

R 9-9

Volume is the amount of space inside an object.
Use cubes to measure volume.

Count how many cubes fill this box.

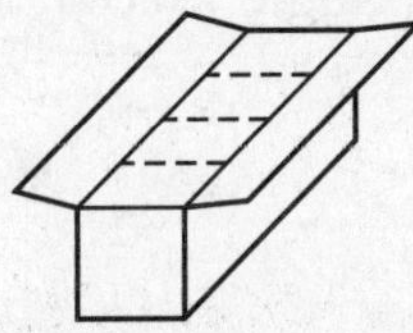

4 cubes

The volume of the box is 4 cubic units.

How many cubes fill each box?
Circle the answers.

1. 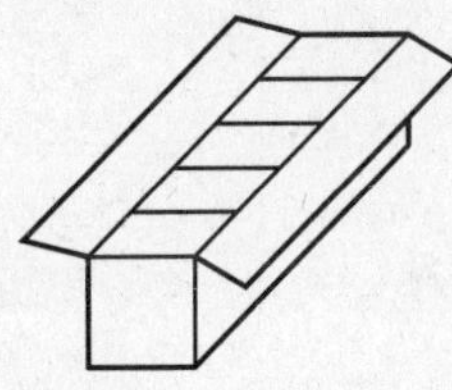

4 cubes   5 cubes

2. 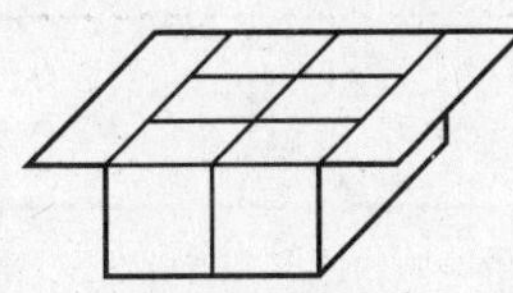

6 cubes   7 cubes

3. 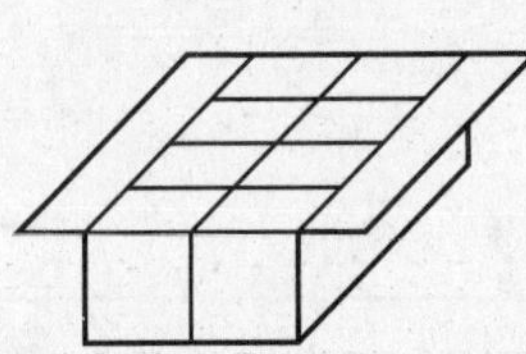

7 cubes   8 cubes

4. 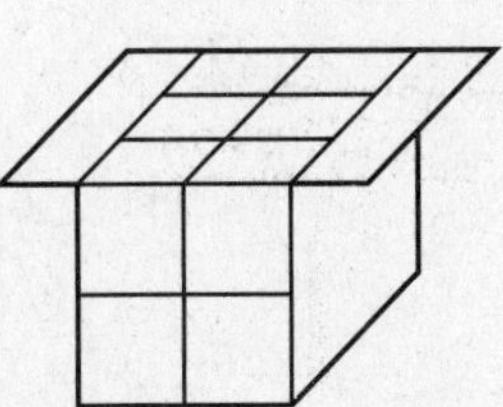

6 cubes   12 cubes

Name ______________________________

Understanding Weight

R 9-10

Weight tells how heavy something is. You can use a balance scale to measure weight. The balance scale shows which object is heavier. The heavier object weighs more and is lower on the scale.

The heavier side of the scale is lower.

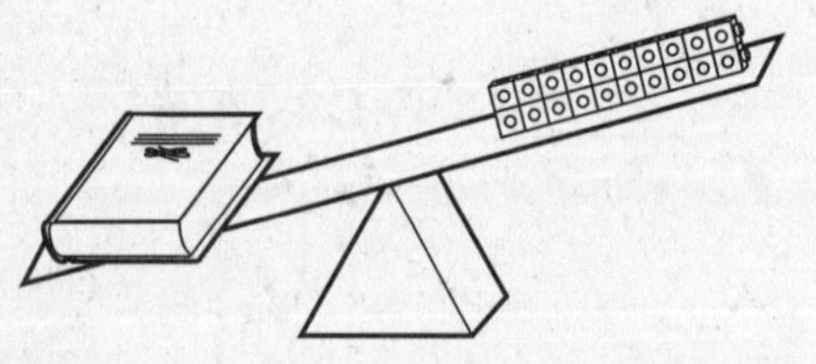

The book weighs more.

The cubes weigh less.

Look at the balance scale.
Then circle the object that weighs more.

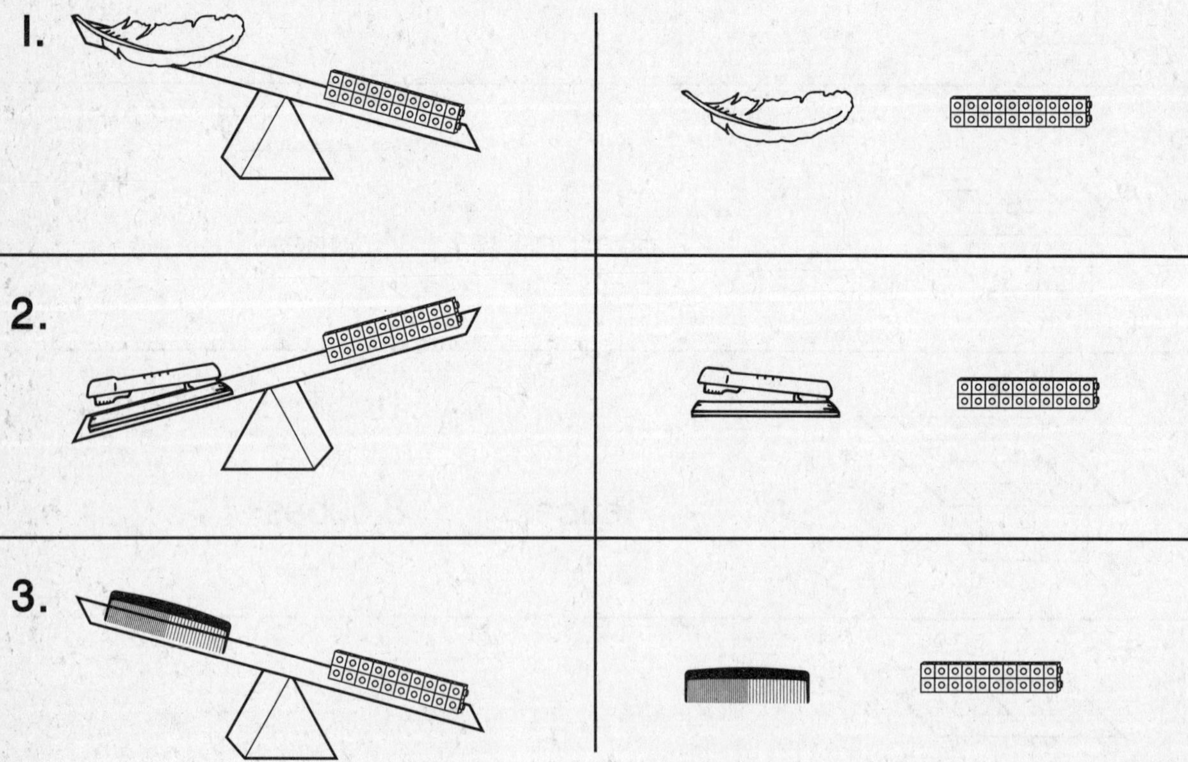

Name ______________________________

Pounds and Ounces

R 9-11

Ounces are used to measure light things.
Pounds are used to measure heavier things.

Remember:
1 pound = 16 ounces.

The book weighs about 1 pound.

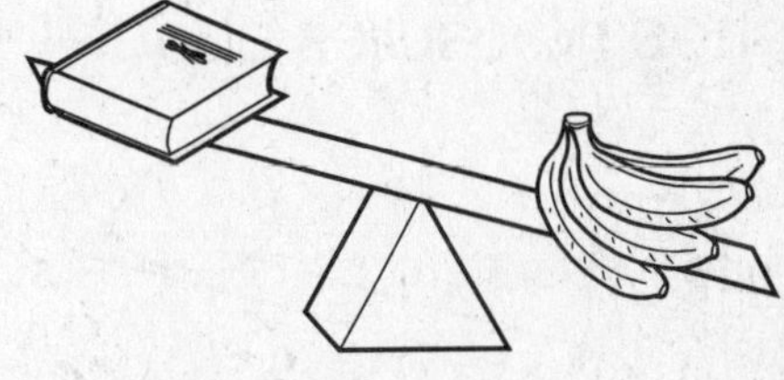

The apple weighs

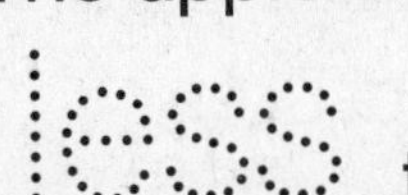

than 1 pound.

The bananas weigh

than 1 pound.

1. Circle the objects that weigh more than 1 pound.

2. Circle the objects that weigh less than 1 pound.

Name ____________________

Grams and Kilograms

R 9-12

Grams are used to measure light things.
Kilograms are used to measure heavier things.

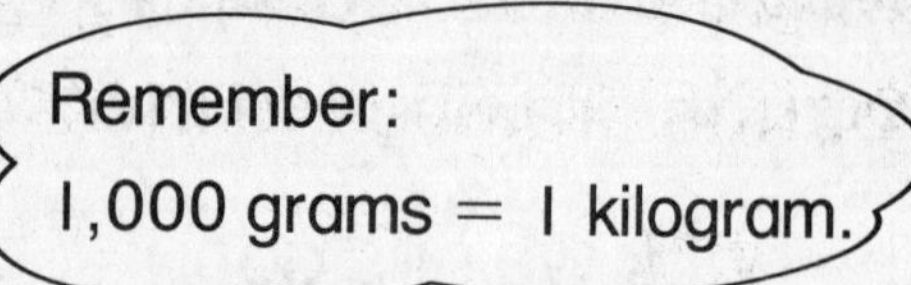

The shoe measures about 1 kilogram.

The balloon measures

than 1 kilogram.

The clock measures

than 1 kilogram.

1. Circle the objects that measure more than 1 kilogram.

2. Circle the objects that measure less than 1 kilogram.

Name ______________________________

Temperature: Fahrenheit and Celsius

R 9-13

Temperature tells how hot or how cold.
You can measure temperature in **Fahrenheit**.

You can also measure temperature in **Celsius**.

Circle **hot** or **cold** to tell about the temperature.

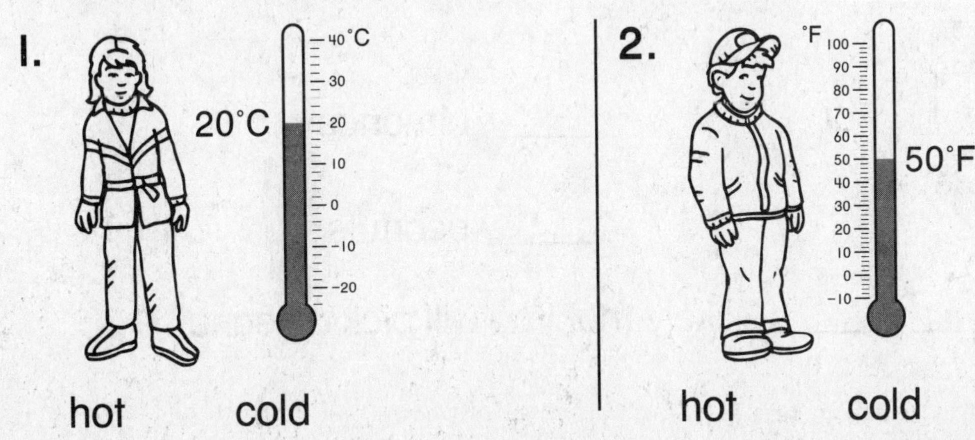

Name ____________________

Understanding Probability

R 9-14

Probability is when you predict if something is **more likely** or **less likely** to happen.

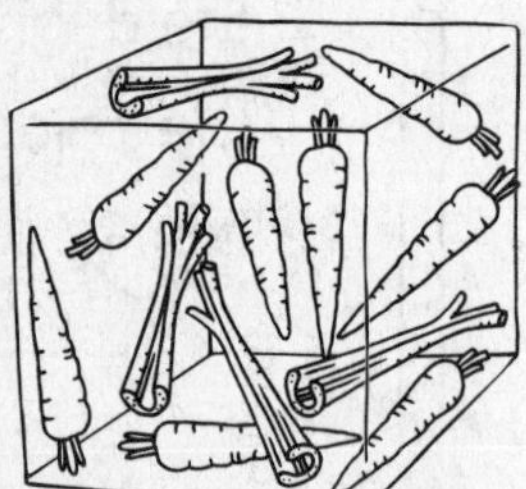

4 celery stalks

8 carrots

Since 8 is greater than 4, it is more likely that you will pick a carrot.

It is more likely that you will pick a carrot.

It is less likely that you will pick a celery stalk.

Write how many of each.
Then write more or less to complete the sentences.

1. 

_____ apples

_____ pears

It is ______________ likely that you will pick a pear.

2. 

_____ almonds

_____ peanuts

It is ______________ likely that you will pick a peanut.

Name ____________________

Using Probability

R 9-15

Words like **certain, probable,** and **impossible** tell about probability.

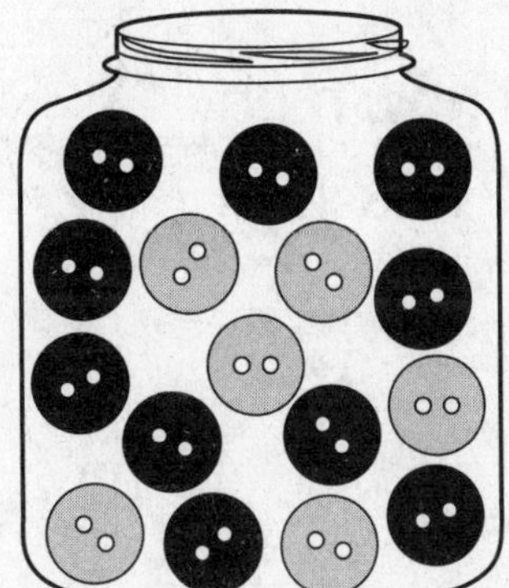

You pick one button from the jar.

It is certain that you will pick a black or a gray button.

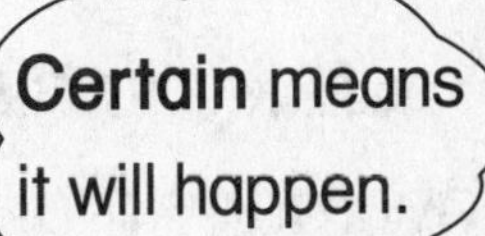

There are more black buttons.

It is probable that you will pick a black button.

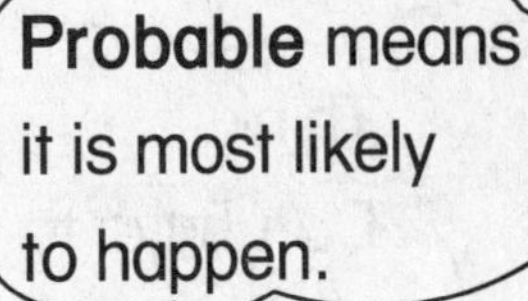

There are not any white buttons.

It is impossible that you will pick a white button.

Impossible means that it will not happen.

Look at the number of buttons in the jar.
Circle the button or buttons that tell about each probability.

You pick one button from the jar.

1. It is **certain** that you will pick

2. It is **probable** that you will pick

3. It is **impossible** that you will pick

Name ____

PROBLEM-SOLVING SKILL **R 9-16**

Multiple-Step Problems

Sometimes it takes two steps to solve a problem.

Timmy has 7 red marbles and 8 blue marbles. He gives 6 marbles to his little brother. How many marbles does Timmy have left?

Think:
Do I have to add or subtract?

Step 1

Add to find out how many marbles Timmy has in all.

Step 2

Subtract to find how many marbles are left.

15 − 6 = 9

Timmy has __9__ marbles left.

Write a number sentence for each part of the problem.
Then write the answer.

1. Sandy picks 8 red flowers and 9 pink flowers.

   She gives 3 flowers to Ben. How many flowers does Sandy have left?

Step 1

Add to find how many flowers she has in all.

____

Step 2

Subtract to find how many flowers Sandy has left.

____

Sandy has _____ flowers left.

Name ____________________

PROBLEM-SOLVING APPLICATIONS **R 9-17**

How Do You Measure Up?

You can use pounds to measure how heavy or how light something is.

The box of blocks weighs more than the book.

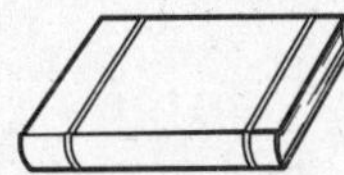

The book weighs about 1 pound.

The box of blocks is ________ 1 pound. less than (more than)

The eraser is ________ 1 pound. (less than) more than

Is it more or less than 1 pound?
Circle your estimate. Then measure.

	Estimate.	Measure.
1.	less than more than	less than more than
2.	less than more than	less than more than

Writing in Math

3. Choose an object in your classroom.
Estimate and measure how much it weighs.
Write about what you find.

____

____

Name ____________________

Building 1,000

R 10-1

Remember.

10 ones = ______ ten

10 tens = ______ hundred

10 hundreds = ______ thousand

Count by 100s to count hundreds.

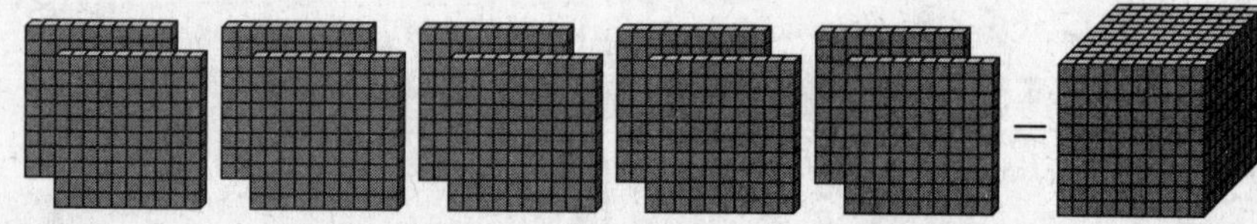

Color the models to show the hundreds.

1. 2 hundreds
200

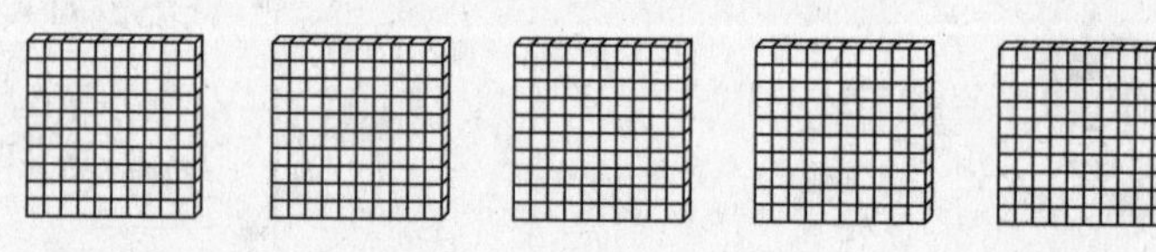

2. 3 hundreds
300

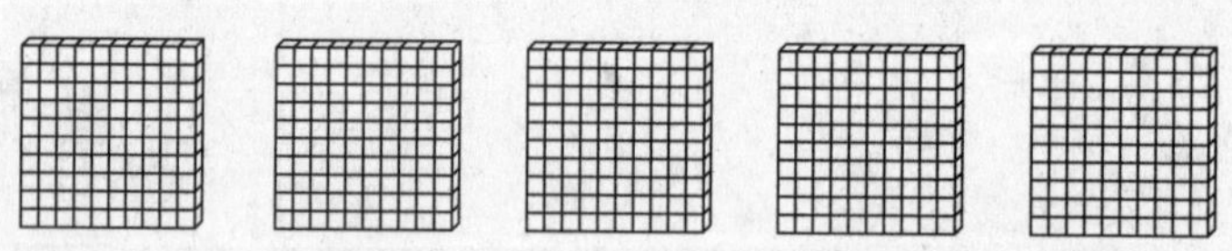

3. 4 hundreds
400

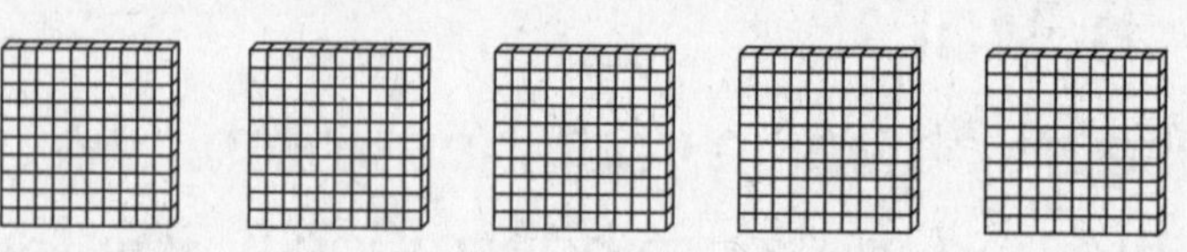

4. 5 hundreds
500

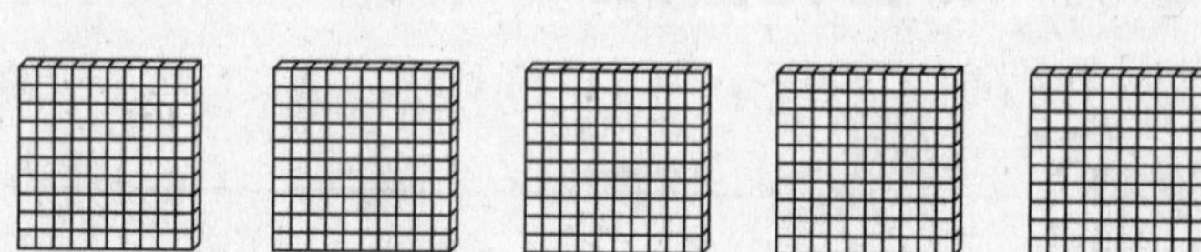

Name ______________________________

Counting Hundreds, Tens, and Ones

You can write a 3-digit number counting hundreds, tens, and ones.

Count the hundreds. Count the tens. Count the ones.

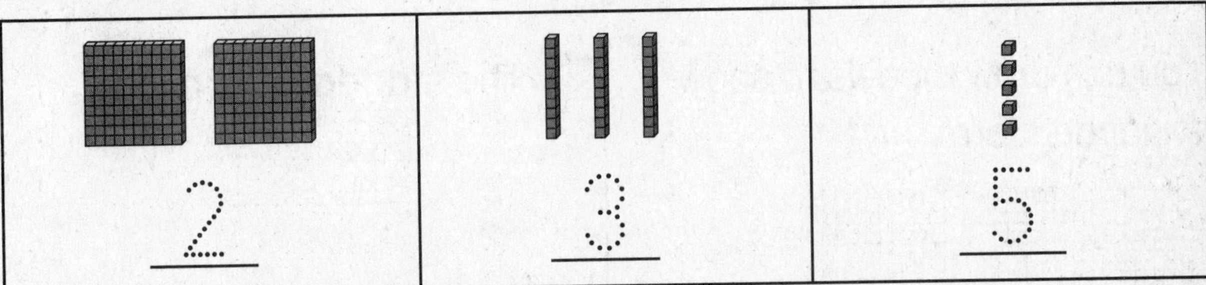

Hundreds	Tens	Ones
2	3	5

The number is 235.

Count the hundreds, tens, and ones. Write the number.

1. 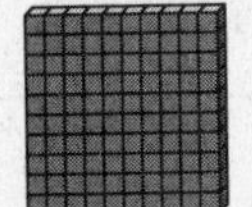 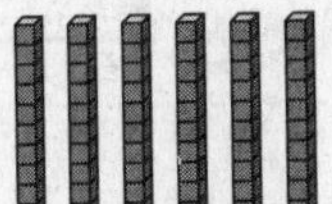 

Hundreds	Tens	Ones

The number is ______.

2. 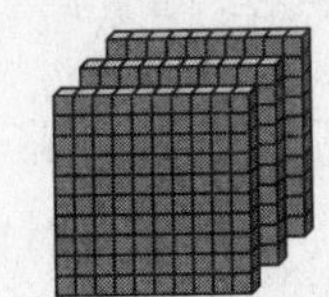 

Hundreds	Tens	Ones

The number is ______.

3. A number has a 5 in the hundreds digit. It has a 9 in the tens digit. It has a 2 in the ones digit. What is the number?

Hundreds	Tens	Ones

The number is ______.

Name ______________________________

Writing Numbers to 1,000

R 10-3

Expanded form uses plus signs to show hundreds, tens, and ones.

200 + 60 + 4

You can draw models to show expanded form.

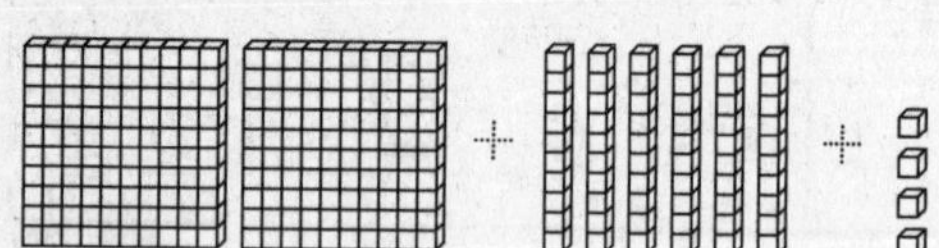

The **number word** is two hundred sixty-four.

The **standard form** is 264.

Draw models to show the expanded form.
Write the number in standard form.

1. 400 + 30 + 8 four hundred thirty-eight

____

2. 300 + 70 + 2 three hundred seventy-two

____

3. 500 + 10 + 4 five hundred fourteen

____

Name ______________________

R 10-4

Changing Numbers by Hundreds and Tens

When you change a number by adding or subtracting tens, only the tens digit changes.

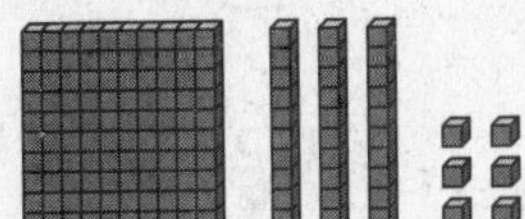

100 + 30 + 6 = 136

Think: 10 more

136 + 10 = 146

Think: 20 less

136 − 20 = 116

When you change a number by adding or subtracting hundreds, only the hundreds digit changes.

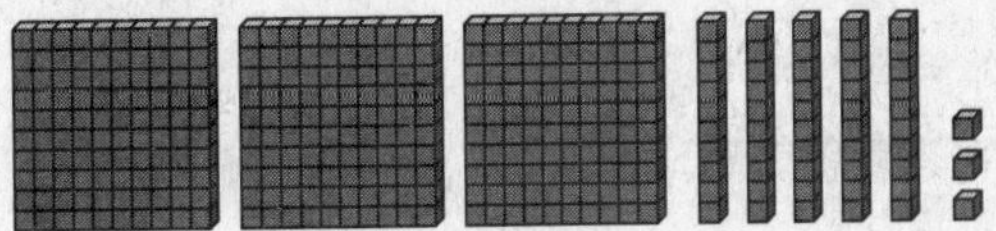

300 + 50 + 3 = 353

Think: 100 more

353 + 100 = 453

Think: 200 less

353 − 200 = 153

Underline the digits that change. Then solve the problem.

1. 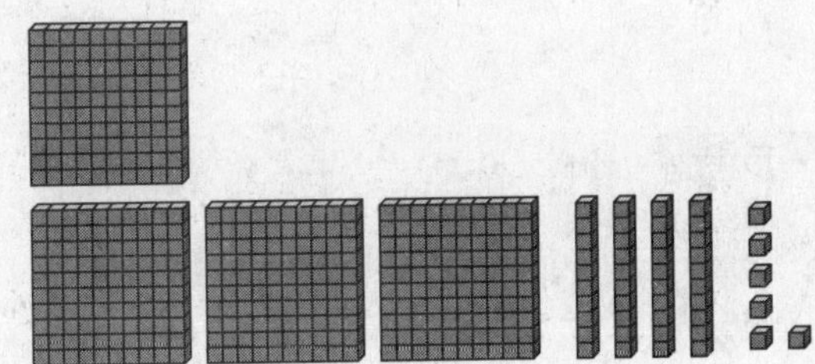

400 + 40 + 6 = 446

446 + 20 = ______

446 + 200 = ______

2. 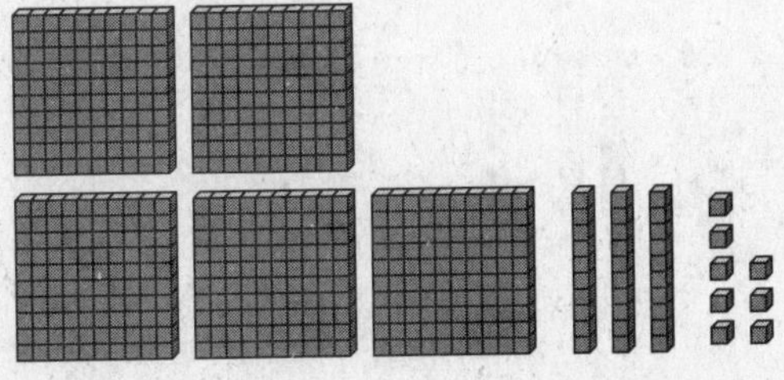

500 + 30 + 8 = 538

538 − 30 = ______

538 − 300 = ______

Name ______________________________

Comparing Numbers

To compare two numbers with unequal hundreds, compare the hundreds first.

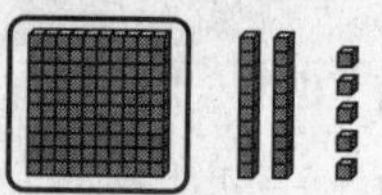

125

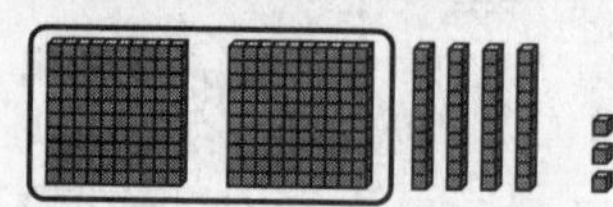

243

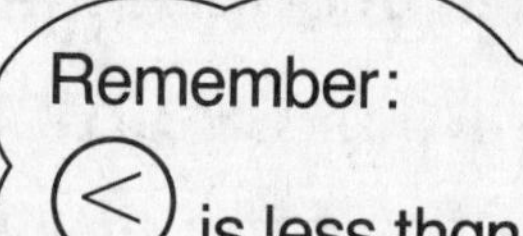

Think: 1 hundred is less than 2 hundreds. So, 125 (<) 243.

To compare two numbers with equal hundreds, compare the tens first.

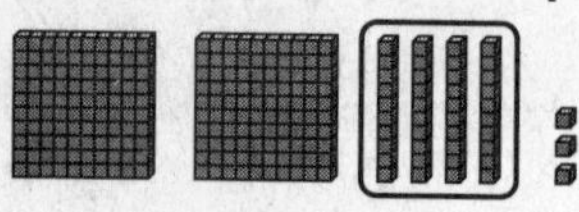

243

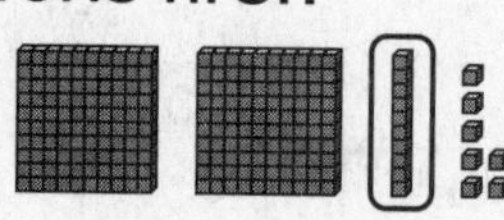

217

Think: 4 tens is greater than 1 ten. So, 243 (>) 217.

Write the number in standard form.
Then compare. Write > or <.

1. 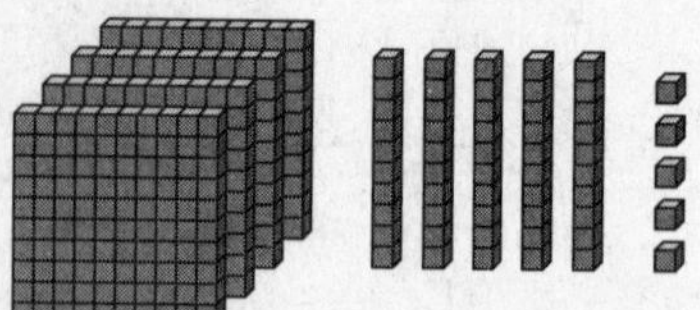 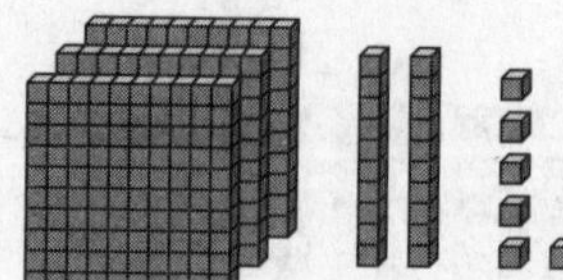

_____ ◯ _____

2. 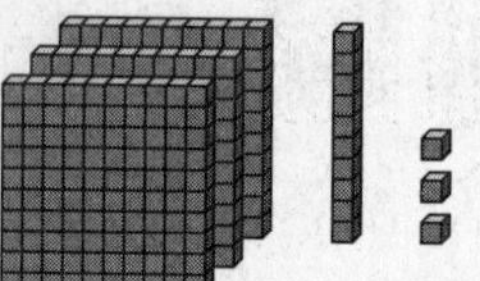

_____  _____

Name ________________________________

Parts of 1,000

R 10-6

There are different ways to make 1,000.

You can count on by 100s and by 10s to make 1,000.

Start with 650.

Count on by 100s.

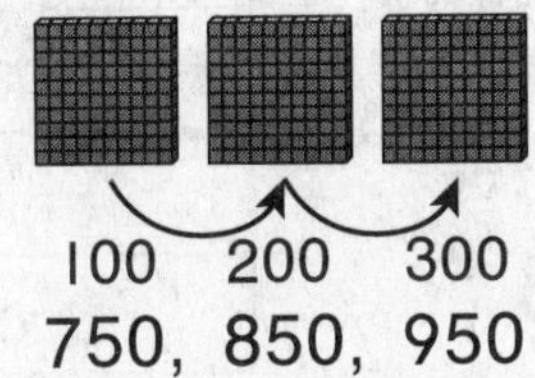

750, 850, 950

Count on by 10s.

10 20 30 40 50

960, 970, 980, 990, 1,000

650 + 300 + 50 = 1,000

650 + 350 = 1,000

Find the parts for 1,000.

Count on by 100s. Then count on by 10s.

1. Start with 750.

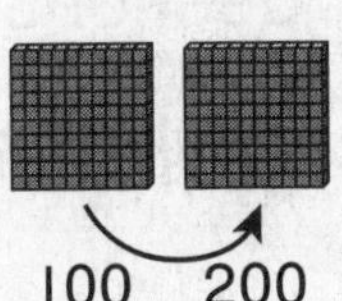

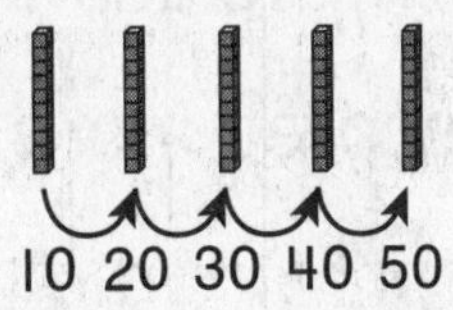

750 + ______ + ______ = 1,000

750 + ______ = 1,000

2. Start with 500.

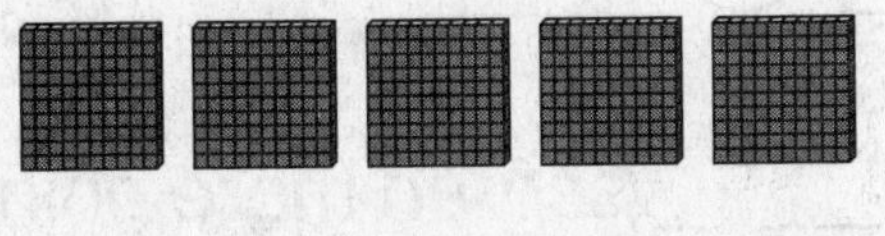

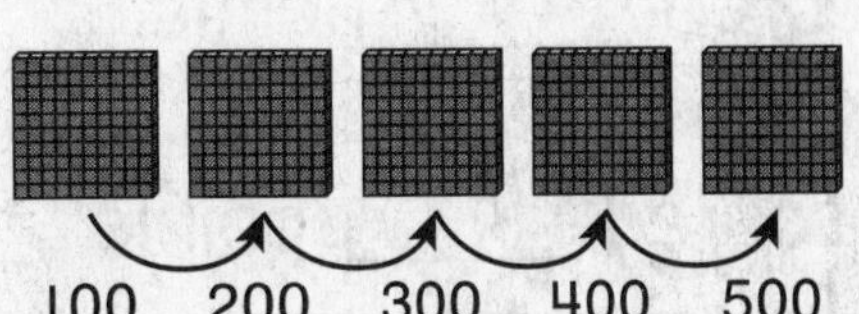

500 + ______ = 1,000

Name ____________________

PROBLEM-SOLVING SKILL **R 10-7**

Use Data from a Chart

You can use a chart to solve problems. This chart shows the points scored on a video game.

Points Scored	
Dan	356
Naomi	617
Philip	582
Lucy	298

Who scored more points, Dan or Naomi?

Look at the chart for the points that Dan and Naomi scored.

Dan scored <u>356</u> points.

Naomi scored <u>617</u> points.

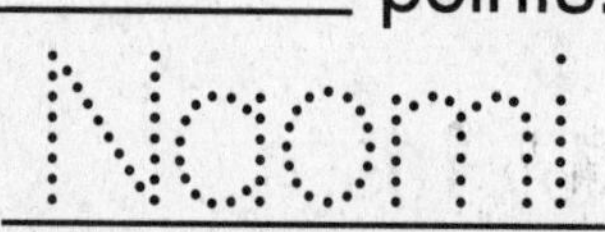

356 (<) 617 <u>Naomi</u> scored more points.

Use the chart to answer the questions.

1. Who scored more points, Philip or Lucy?

Philip scored ______ points. ______ ◯ ______

Lucy scored ______ points. __________ scored more points.

2. Who scored more points, Lucy or Naomi?

Lucy scored ______ points. ______ ◯ ______

Naomi scored ______ points. __________ scored more points.

3. Who scored 300 + 50 + 6 points? __________

Name ______________________________

Before, After, and Between

R 10-8

Think about the order of numbers.

150	151	152	153	154	155	156	157	158	159
160	161	162	163	164	165	166	167	168	169

152 is **before** 153.  168 is **after** 167.

 161 is **between** 160 and 162.

Write the numbers that are before, after, and between.

1.

300	301	302	303	304	305	306	307	308	309
310	311	312	313	314	315	316	317	318	319

______ is **before** 314. ______ is **after** 304.

______ is **between** 303 and 305.

2.

750	751	752	753	754	755	756	757	758	759
760	761	762	763	764	765	766	767	768	769

______ is **before** 765. ______ is **after** 758.

______ is **between** 752 and 754.

3.

530	531	532	533	534	535	536	537	538	539
540	541	542	543	544	545	546	547	548	549

______ is **before** 549. ______ is **after** 530.

______ is **between** 541 and 543.

Name ______________________________

Ordering Numbers

R 10-9

These numbers are in order from least to greatest.

$167 < 270 < 273 < 499$

Each number is less than ($<$) the number after it.

These numbers are in order from greatest to least.

$684 > 680 > 371 > 262$

Each number is greater than ($>$) the number after it.

Order the numbers from least to greatest.

275 543 110 212

$110 < 212 < 275 < 543$

Order the numbers from greatest to least.

616 583 775 102

$775 > 616 > 583 > 102$

Write the numbers in order from least to greatest.

1. 187 126 219 267 ______, ______, ______, ______

2. 341 489 452 317 ______, ______, ______, ______

Write the numbers in order from greatest to least.

3. 419 578 535 487 ______, ______, ______, ______

4. 682 734 546 650 ______, ______, ______, ______

Name ____________________

PROBLEM-SOLVING STRATEGY **R 10-10**

Look for a Pattern

A pattern is something that repeats.

Read and Understand

Look for a pattern rule to find what number comes next.
What number comes next? 280, 270, 260, 250, 240, ___?___

Plan and Solve

Think. What digit changes? 280, 270, 260, 250, 240 ___10s___

Think. Does it increase or decrease? 280, 270, 260, 250, 240 ___decrease___

Think. By how much? 280, 270, 260, 250, 240 ___by 10___

The pattern rule is ___The numbers decrease by 10.___

The next number is ___230___.

Look Back and Check

Does your answer fit the pattern rule?

Write the numbers that come next. Describe the pattern rule.

1. 285, 385, 485, 585, 685, ______, ______, ______

The pattern rule is: ____________________

2. 340, 360, 380, 400, 420, ______, ______, ______

The pattern rule is: ____________________

Name ______________________________

PROBLEM-SOLVING APPLICATIONS **R 10-11**

Rescue Vehicles

Fire truck A has 600 gallons of water. Fire truck B has 100 more gallons.

Fire truck A: 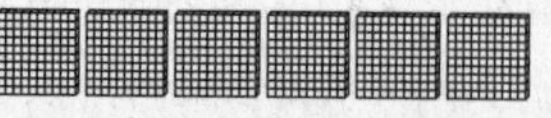

Fire truck B: 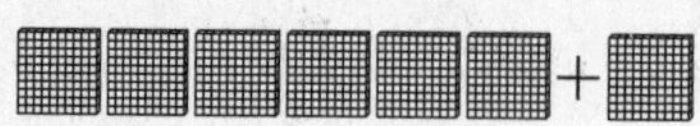

600 + 100 = 700

100 more than 600 is

700 gallons.

Fire truck C has 500 gallons of water. It uses 100 gallons to put out a fire.

Fire truck C: 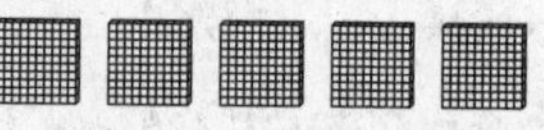

Gallons used: 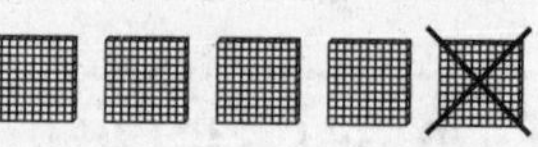

500 − 100 = 400

100 less than 500 is

400 gallons.

Solve.

1. A firefighter goes on 30 calls in one month.
   How much is 10 calls less than that?

   30 − 10 = _____ calls

   How much is 10 calls more than that?

   30 + 10 = _____ calls

2. A fire truck travels 400 miles in one month.
   How much is 100 miles more than that? _____ miles

   How much is 100 miles less than that? _____ miles

Name ________________________________

Using Mental Math

R 11-1

Add 315 + 264. Use mental math.

To add using mental math, begin with the expanded form of each number. Then add each place value.

315 → 300 + 10 + 5
264 → + 200 + 60 + 4
500 + 70 + 9

500 + 70 + 9 = 579

So, 315 + 264 = 579

Add.

1. 523 + 172 = ?

523 → 500 + 20 + 3
172 → + 100 + 70 + 2
600 + 90 + 5

600 + 90 + 5 = 695

So, 523 + 172 = 695

2. 281 + 716 = ?

281 → ____ + ____ + ____
716 → + ____ + ____ + ____
____ + ____ + ____

____ + ____ + ____ = ____

So, 281 + 716 = ____

3. 193 + 605 = ?

193 → ____ + ____ + ____
605 → + ____ + ____ + ____
____ + ____ + ____

____ + ____ + ____ = ____

So, 193 + 605 = ____

Name ______________________________

Estimating Sums

R 11-2

You can estimate to find an answer that is close to the exact sum. To estimate, find the closest hundred.

Estimate 185 + 437. Is it more than or less than 500?

Is 185 closer to 100 or 200? 200

Is 437 closer to 400 or 500? 400

200 + 400 = 600

So, 185 + 437 is more than 500.

Is the sum more or less than the number?
Estimate the sum. Write **more than** or **less than.**

1. Is 179 + 267 more than or less than 600?

   179 is close to _____. 267 is close to _____.

   _____ + _____ = _____.

   179 + 267 is ____________________ 600.

2. Is 327 + 417 more than or less than 600?

   327 is close to _____. 417 is close to _____.

   _____ + _____ = _____.

   327 + 417 is ____________________ 600.

Name ____________________

Adding with Models

R 11-3

135 + 248 = ____

Step 1: Add the ones. Regroup if you need to.

Step 2: Add the tens. Regroup if you need to.

Step 3: Add the hundreds.

	Hundreds	Tens	Ones
135			
248			

5 + 8 = 13 ones. Regroup 10 ones for 1 ten.

135 + 248 = 383

Add to find the sum. Use models and Workmat 5.
Show each number.

1.

Hundreds	Tens	Ones

341 + 127 = ____

2.

Hundreds	Tens	Ones

524 + 249 = ____

Name ____________________

Adding Three-Digit Numbers

R 11-4

Step 1: Add the ones. Regroup if you need to.
Step 2: Add the tens. Regroup if you need to.
Step 3: Add the hundreds.

Think:
Regroup 10 tens for 1 hundred.

163 + 174 = ___?___

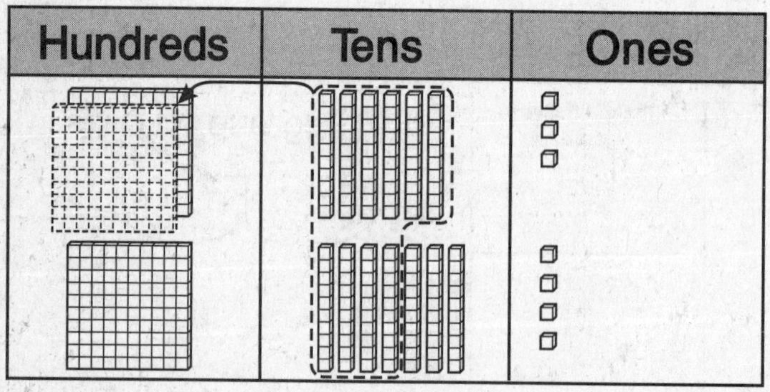

Hundreds	Tens	Ones
1		
1	6	3
+ 1	7	4
3	3	7

Draw to regroup. Add.

1. 218 + 136 = ___?___

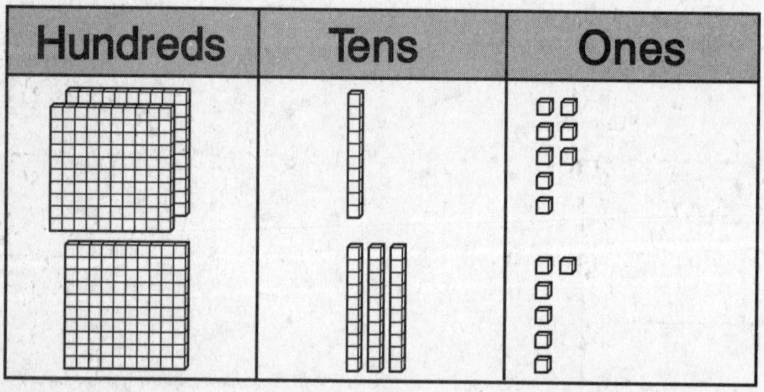

Hundreds	Tens	Ones
2	1	8
+ 1	3	6

Add. Use models and Workmat 5 if you need to.

2.

Hundreds	Tens	Ones
1	2	5
+ 2	4	2

3.

Hundreds	Tens	Ones
4	1	9
+ 2	5	6

Name ______________________________

Practice with Three-Digit Addition

R 11-5

417 + 163 = ?

Rewrite the problem using the workmat.

Line up the hundreds, tens, and ones.

1. Add the ones. Regroup if you need to.
2. Add the tens. Regroup if you need to.
3. Add the hundreds.

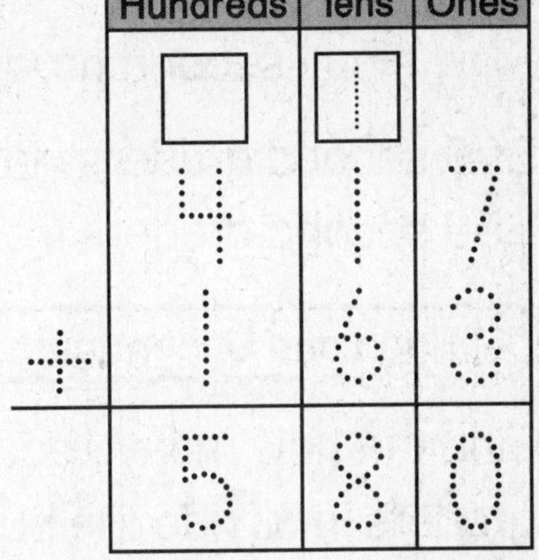

Write the addition problem. Find the sum.

1. 152 + 341

	Hundreds	Tens	Ones
	☐	☐	
	1	5	2
+	3	4	1
	4	9	3

374 + 183

	Hundreds	Tens	Ones
	☐	☐	
+			

560 + 278

	Hundreds	Tens	Ones
	☐	☐	
+			

2. 415 + 142

	Hundreds	Tens	Ones
	☐	☐	
+			

192 + 173

	Hundreds	Tens	Ones
	☐	☐	
+			

307 + 378

	Hundreds	Tens	Ones
	☐	☐	
+			

Name ______________________________

PROBLEM-SOLVING STRATEGY **R 11-6**

Make a Graph

How many second graders ride the bus?

200 second graders from Willow Town ride the bus.
250 second graders from Dandy Creek ride the bus.

Read and Understand

Find out how many second graders in all ride the bus.

Plan and Solve

First, add the number of second graders from both towns.

$$\begin{array}{r} 200 \\ +\ 250 \\ \hline 450 \end{array}$$

450 second graders ride the bus.

Then, add this information to the graph.

Children Riding the Bus

	First Graders	Second Graders	Third Graders
650			
600			
550			
500			
450		■	
400		■	
350		■	
300		■	
250		■	
200		■	
150		■	
100		■	
50		■	
0			

Look Back and Check

Does the bar above second graders stop at 450?

Read the problems. Add to find how many in all.
Then complete the graph.

1. 150 first graders from Willow Town ride the bus. 200 first graders from Dandy Creek ride the bus.

   _____ first graders in all.

2. 350 third graders from Willow Town ride the bus. 250 third graders from Dandy Creek ride the bus.

   _____ third graders in all.

Name ______________________________

Ways to Find Missing Parts

R 11-7

Count on by hundreds and tens to find the parts of the whole.

260 + _____ = 700

First, count on by hundreds. 4 hundreds

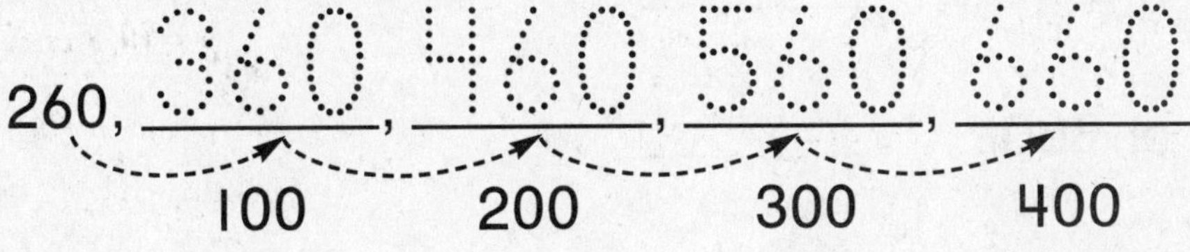

Next, count on by tens. 4 tens

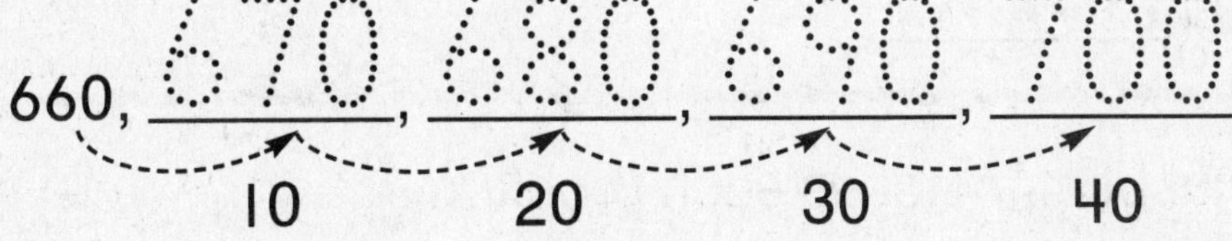

4 hundreds and 4 tens is 440.

So, 260 + 440 = 700

700	
260	440

I. 350 + ? = 600

Count on by hundreds. _____ hundreds

350, _____, _____

Count on by tens. _____ tens

550, _____, _____, _____, _____, _____

_____ hundreds and _____ tens is _____.

So, 350 + _____ = 600

Name ______________________

Estimating Differences

R 11-8

You can estimate to find an answer that is close to the exact difference. To estimate, find the closest hundred.

Estimate 596 − 221.

Is 596 closer to 500 or 600? 600

Is 221 closer to 200 or 300? 200

600 − 200 = 400

So, 596 − 221 is about 400.

Circle the estimate that best matches each problem.

1. 502 − 105	is about	200	300	400
2. 909 − 403	is about	500	600	700
3. 615 − 412	is about	100	200	300
4. 511 − 298	is about	200	300	400
5. 881 − 500	is about	300	400	500
6. 231 − 108	is about	100	200	300
7. 799 − 182	is about	400	500	600
8. 627 − 275	is about	200	300	400

Name ______________________________

Subtracting with Models

R 11-9

327 − 164 = __?__

Step 1: Subtract the ones. Regroup if you need to.

Step 2: Subtract the tens. Regroup if you need to.

Step 3: Subtract the hundreds.

Hundreds	Tens	Ones

327 − 164 = __163__

Subtract to find the difference. Use models and Workmat 5.
Show each number.

1.

Hundreds	Tens	Ones

549 − 295 = ______

2.

Hundreds	Tens	Ones

835 − 516 = ______

Name ______________________________

Subtracting Three-Digit Numbers

R 11-10

Step 1: Subtract the ones. Regroup if you need to.
Step 2: Subtract the tens. Regroup if you need to.
Step 3: Subtract the hundreds.

Think: Regroup 1 ten for 10 ones.

362 − 125 = ___?___

Hundreds	Tens	Ones
	5	12
3	~~6~~	~~2~~
− 1	2	5
2	3	7

Draw to regroup. Subtract.

1. 429 − 174 = ___?___

Hundreds	Tens	Ones
4	2	9
− 1	7	4

Subtract. Use models and Workmat 5 if you need to.

2.

Hundreds	Tens	Ones
5	7	4
− 2	1	3

3.

Hundreds	Tens	Ones
7	8	8
− 2	6	9

Name ______________________________

Practice with Three-Digit Subtraction

R 11-11

528 − 143 = ___?___

Rewrite the problem using the workmat.

Line up the hundreds, tens, and ones.

Subtract the ones. Regroup if you need to.

Subtract the tens. Regroup if you need to.

Subtract the hundreds.

	Hundreds	Tens	Ones
	4	12	
	~~5~~	~~2~~	8
−	1	4	3
	3	8	5

Write the subtraction problem. Find the difference.

1. 648 − 217

	Hundreds	Tens	Ones
	6	4	8
−	2	1	7
	4	3	1

593 − 264

	Hundreds	Tens	Ones
−			

435 − 192

	Hundreds	Tens	Ones
−			

2. 328 − 114

	Hundreds	Tens	Ones
−			

782 − 329

	Hundreds	Tens	Ones
−			

957 − 173

	Hundreds	Tens	Ones
−			

Name ____________________

PROBLEM-SOLVING SKILL **R 11-12**

Exact Answer or Estimate

James collects 321 cans for recycling day. He needs 550 cans to win a prize. How many more cans does James need?

Subtract to find the **exact** amount of cans James needs.

$$\begin{array}{r} 550 \\ -\,321 \\ \hline 229 \end{array}$$

229 cans

Genie collects 387 cans. Sandra collects 134 cans. About how many more cans does Genie collect than Sandra?

To find out **about** how many more cans, use an estimate.

387 is about 400
134 is about 100

$$\begin{array}{r} 400 \\ -\,100 \\ \hline 300 \end{array}$$

about 300 more

Circle **estimate** or **exact answer.** Solve.

1. Aleesha collects 327 newspapers. She needs 650 to fill a carton. How many more papers does she need?

exact answer estimate

Subtract to find the answer.

$$\begin{array}{r} 650 \\ -\,327 \\ \hline \end{array}$$

________ more

2. Nan collects 167 plastic bottles. She collects 219 glass bottles. About how many bottles does she collect in all?

exact answer estimate

Add to find the answer.

$$\begin{array}{r} \\ + \quad \\ \hline \end{array}$$

about _____ bottles

Name ____________________

PROBLEM-SOLVING APPLICATIONS R 11-13

Amazing Animals

You can add to solve problems with three-digit numbers.

A tree frog lays 134 eggs.
Another tree frog lays 182 eggs.
How many eggs did they lay in all?

Add to find how many in all.

```
   1
   134
 + 182
 -----
   316  eggs
```

You can subtract to solve problems with three-digit numbers.

A male lion weighs 475 pounds.
A female lion weighs 384 pounds.
How many more pounds does the male weigh?

Subtract to find how many more.

```
  3 17
  4 7 5
- 3 8 4
-------
    9 1  more pounds
```

Solve.

1. A rain forest tree is 238 feet tall.
   Another tree is 172 feet tall.
   How much taller is the first tree?

   Subtract to find the answer.

   ____ feet taller

```
  □ □ □
  2 3 8
-
-------
```

2. A group of tourists travels 387 miles to a rain forest. Then they travel 152 miles through the rain forest.
   How many miles did they travel in all?

   Add to find the answer.

   ____ miles

Name ______________________________

Skip Counting Equal Groups

R 12-1

You can skip count **equal groups** to find how many there are in all.

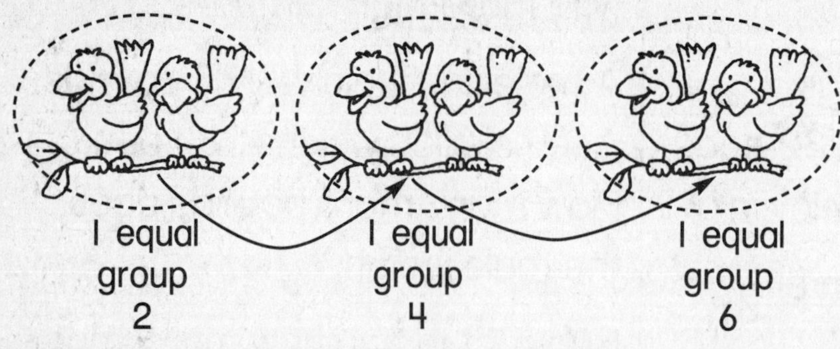

3 equal groups

2 birds in each equal group

6 birds in all

Circle the equal groups.
Skip count to find out how many there are in all.

I.

I equal group I equal group I equal group I equal group

_____ equal groups

_____ flowers in each equal group

_____ flowers in all

2.

_____ equal groups

_____ apples in each equal group

_____ apples in all

3.

_____ equal groups

_____ bananas in each equal group

_____ bananas in all

Name ______________________________

Repeated Addition and Multiplication

R 12-2

You can write an addition sentence
to tell how many there are in all.
You can write a multiplication sentence
to tell how many there are in all.

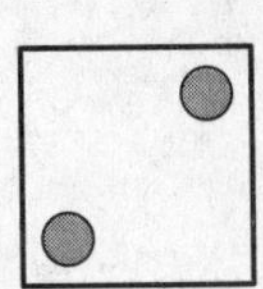 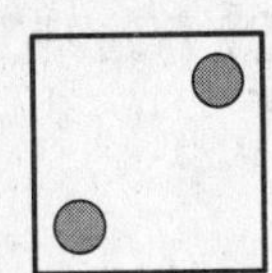 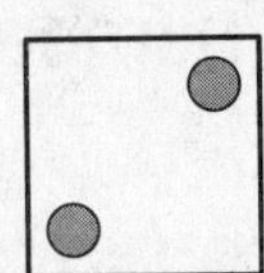 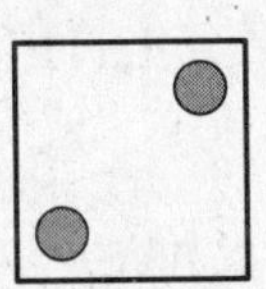

4 equal groups

2 in each group

2 + 2 + 2 + 2 = 8 in all

4 × 2 = 8 in all

Write the number of equal groups.
Write how many there are in each group. Then write
an addition sentence and a multiplication sentence.

1. 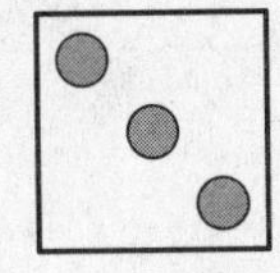 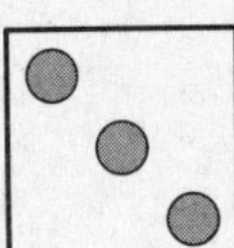 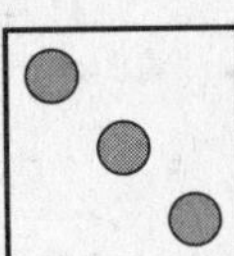 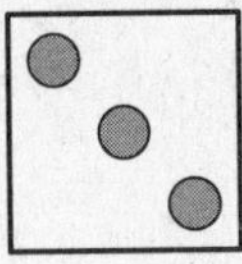 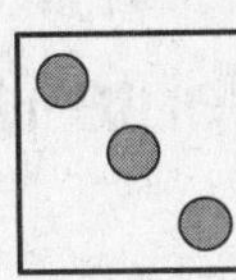

____ equal groups

____ in each group

____ + ____ + ____ + ____ + ____ = ____ in all

____ × ____ = ____ in all

2. 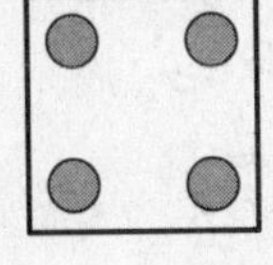 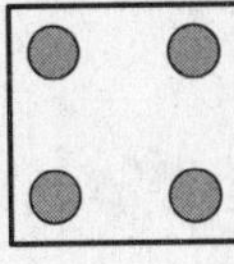 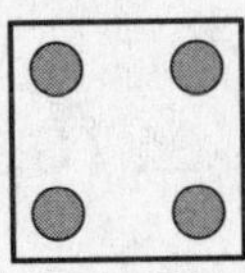 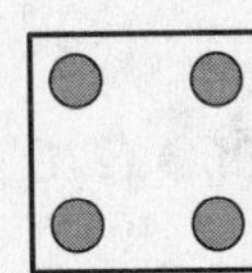

____ equal groups

____ in each group

____ + ____ + ____ + ____ = ____ in all

____ × ____ = ____ in all

Name ______________________________

Building Arrays

R 12-3

A collection of objects arranged in equal rows and columns is an **array.** You can use an **array** to show equal groups.

Array

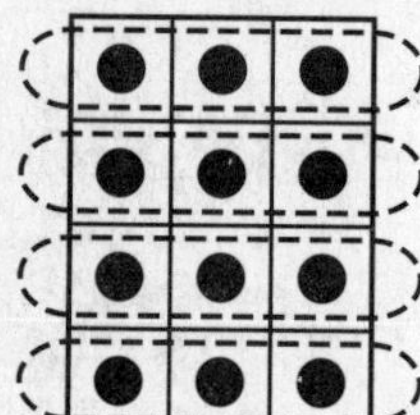

Circle each row. Count the number of rows.

There are __4__ rows.

Count the number of dots in each row.

There are __3__ dots in each row.

Write the multiplication sentence.

__4__ × __3__ = __12__ in all

Circle each row. Count the number of rows.
Count the number of dots in each row.
Write the multiplication sentence.

1.

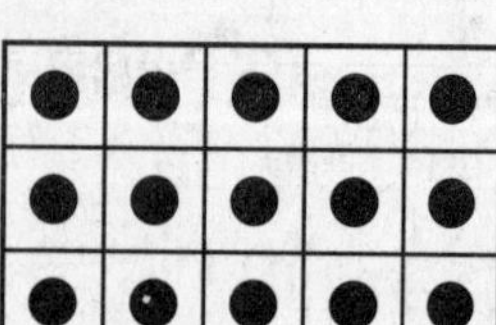

There are ____ rows.

There are ____ dots in each row.

____ × ____ = ____ in all.

2.

There are ____ rows.

There are ____ dots in each row.

____ × ____ = ____ in all.

Name ____________________

Multiplying in Any Order

R 12-4

You can multiply numbers in any order and get the same product.

Color 3 rows with 2 in each row.

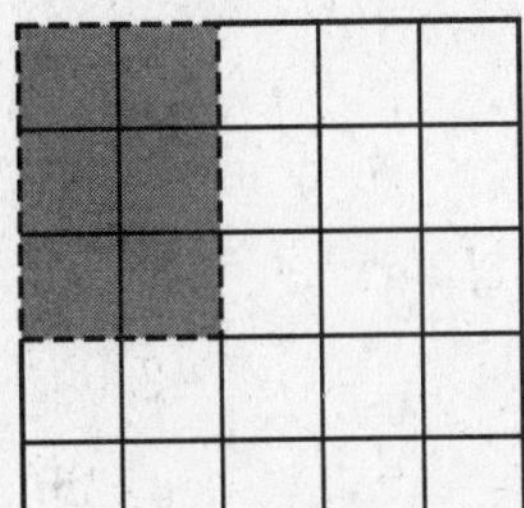

3 × 2 = 6
rows, in each row, in all

Color 2 rows with 3 in each row.

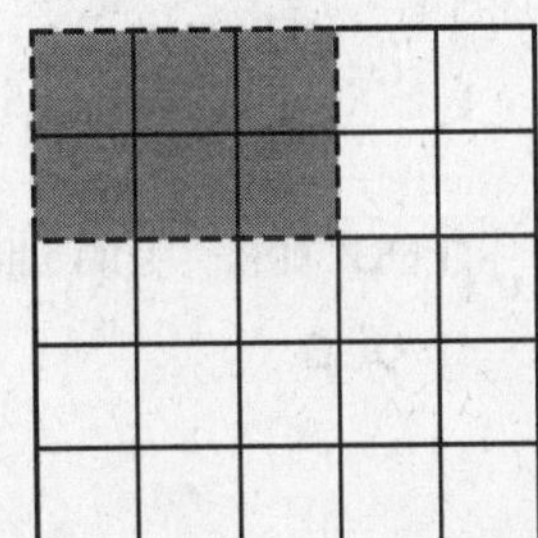

2 × 3 = 6
rows, in each row, in all

So, 3 × 2 is the same as 2 × 3.

Color the rows. Write the numbers.
Multiply to find the product.

1. Color 5 rows with 3 in each row.

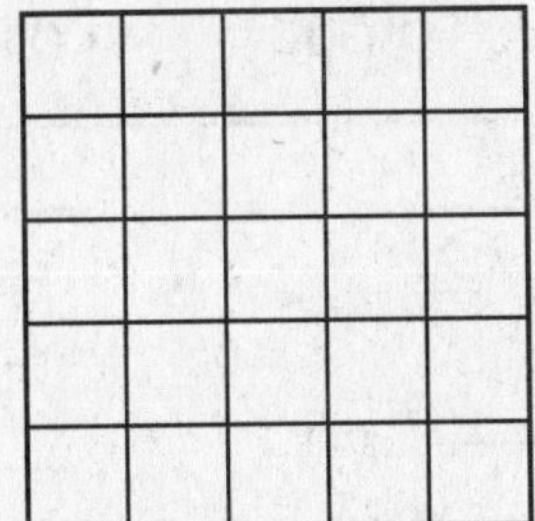

_____ × _____ = _____
rows, in each row, in all

Color 3 rows with 5 in each row.

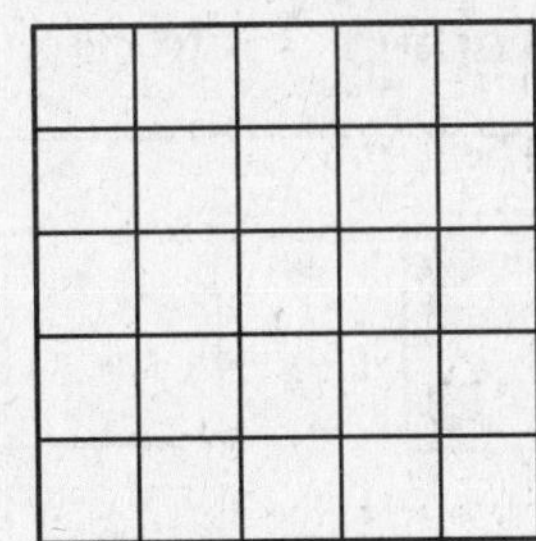

_____ × _____ = _____
rows, in each row, in all

So, _____ × _____ is the same as _____ × _____.

Name ______________________________

Vertical Form

You can write multiplication facts in two ways.

When you multiply down, it is called **vertical** form.

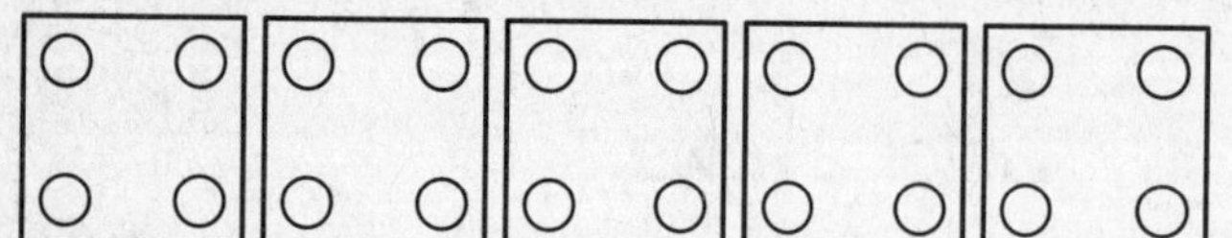

Down

4 in each group

× 5 groups

20 in all

Across 5 × 4 = 20

groups, in each group, in all

Write each multiplication fact two ways.

1. 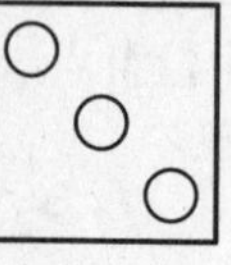 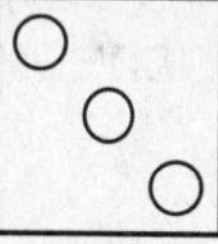 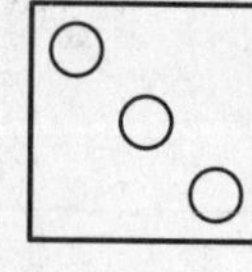 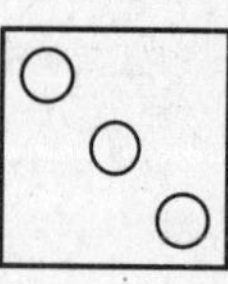

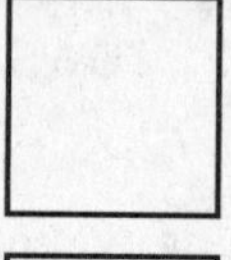 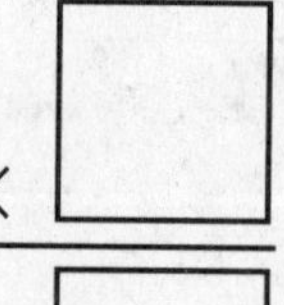

×

____ × ____ = ____

groups, in each group, in all

2. 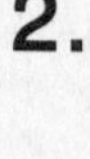 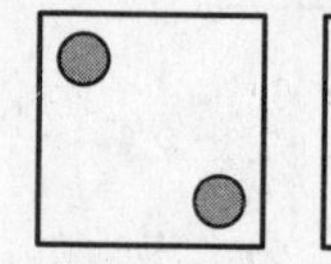 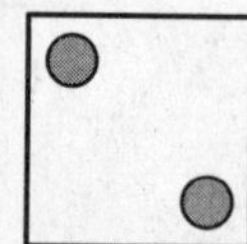 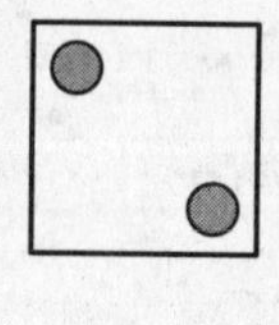 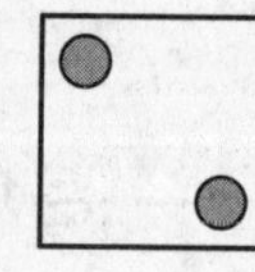 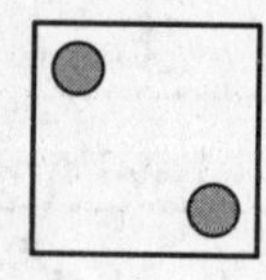

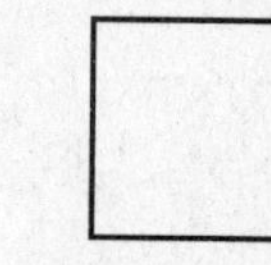 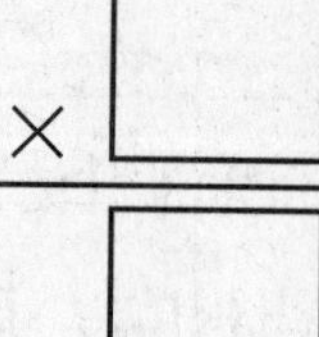

×

____ × ____ = ____

groups, in each group, in all

3. 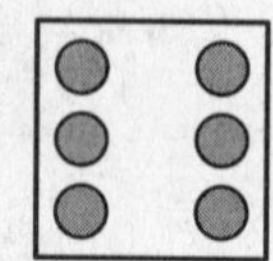 

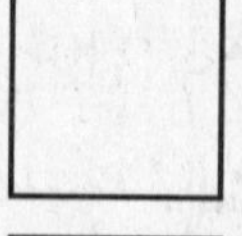 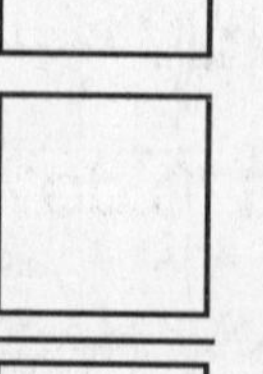 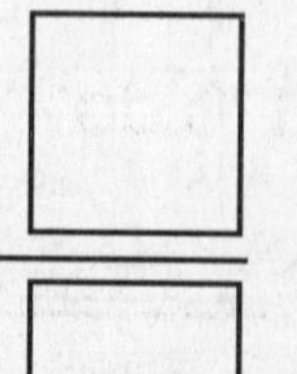

×

____ × ____ = ____

4. 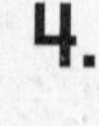 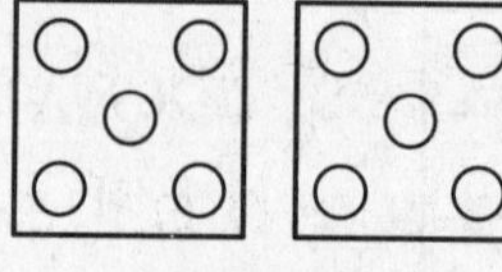 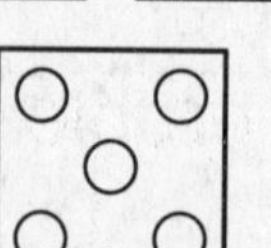

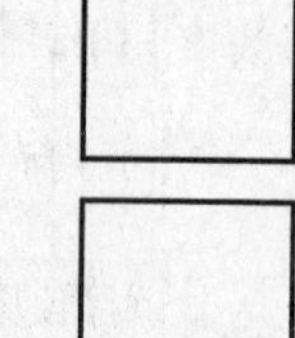 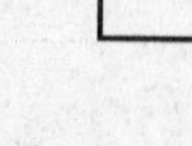

×

____ × ____ = ____

Name ____________________

PROBLEM-SOLVING STRATEGY **R 12-6**

Draw a Picture

You can draw a picture to solve a problem.

Read and Understand

Francis knits 4 mittens. Each mitten has 5 buttons.
How many buttons are there in all?

What does the problem ask you to do?

Find how many buttons in all.

Plan and Solve

There are 4 mittens. Draw 5 buttons on each mitten.

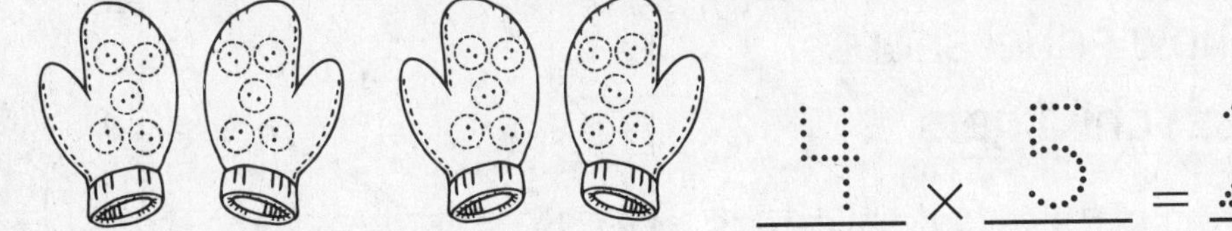

4 × 5 = 20 buttons in all

Look Back and Check

Did you draw the correct number of groups?
Did you use the correct number to show how many in each group? Does the answer make sense?

Draw a picture to solve. Then write a multiplication sentence.

1. There are 6 vases. Each vase has 3 flowers.
How many flowers are there in all?

What does the problem ask you to do?

____

_____ × _____ = _____ flowers in all

Name ____________________

Making Equal Groups

R 12-7

You can share equally by making equal groups.

To make an **equal share,** give each child the same amount.

There are 9 counters in all.
There are 3 children. Draw equal shares.
How many counters does each child get?

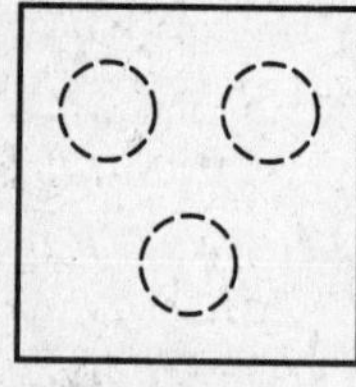

Matthew

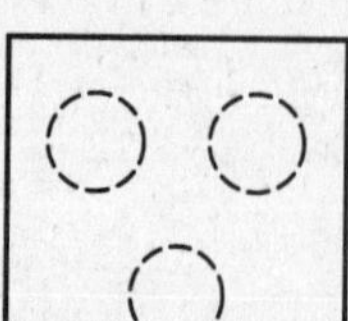

Aliki

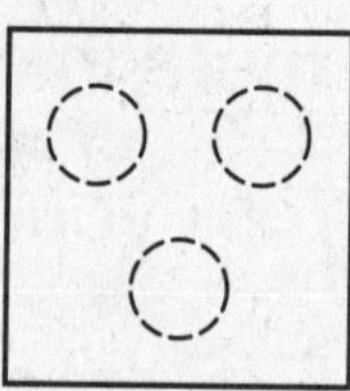

Hannah

Each child gets __3__ counters.

Draw counters to show equal shares.
Write how many each child gets.

1. 4 children want to share 16 counters equally.

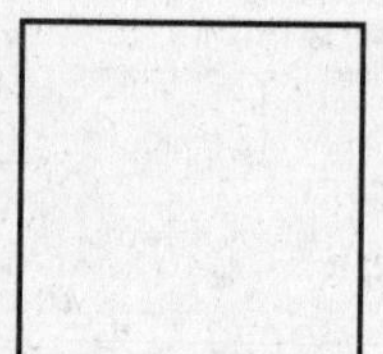

Philip

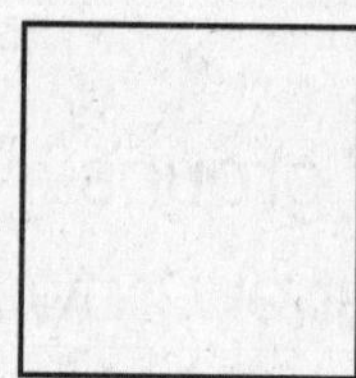

Elizabeth

Beto

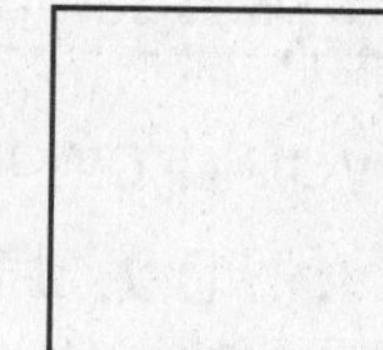

Helen

Each child gets _____ counters.

2. 3 children want to share 15 counters equally.

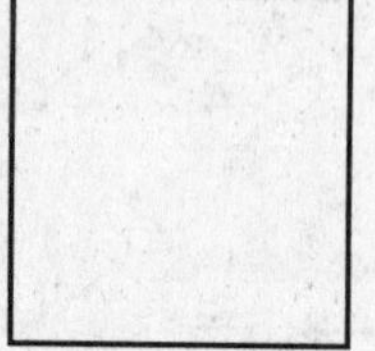

Sabrina

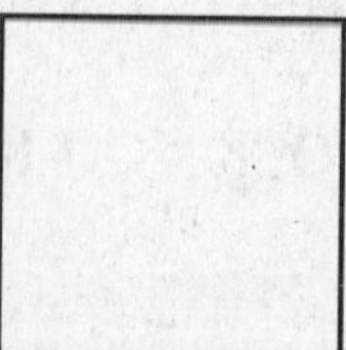

Moesha

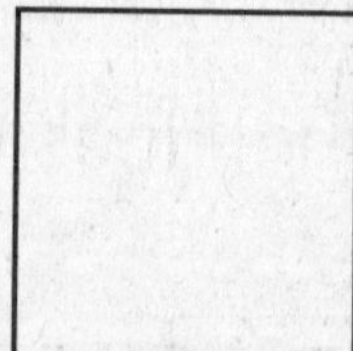

Kyle

Each child gets _____ counters.

Name ______________________________

Writing Division Sentences

R 12-8

When you share equally, you **divide.**

5 children want to share 10 counters equally. Draw 1 counter for each child. Keep drawing 1 counter for each child until you have drawn 10 counters in all.

Brandon

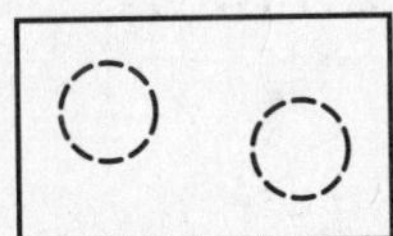

Melissa

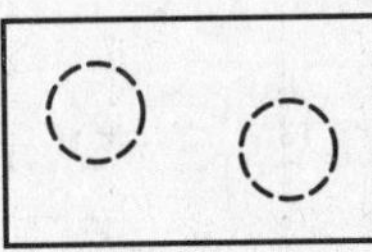

Joaquin

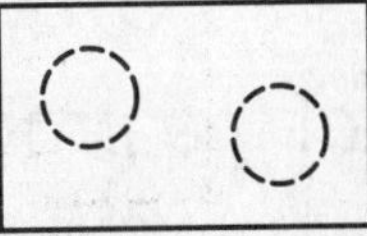

Dorothea

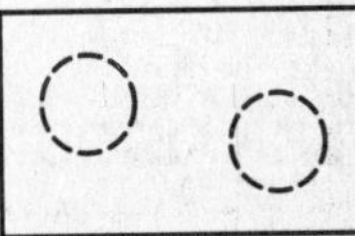

Janet

There are <u>10</u> counters to share equally.

There are <u>5</u> groups of counters.

There are <u>2</u> counters in each group.

Each child gets <u>2</u> counters. So, $10 \div 5 =$ <u>2</u>.

Draw to show equal groups.
Write how many each child gets.
Then write the division sentence.

1. 4 children want to share 12 counters.

Gabriel

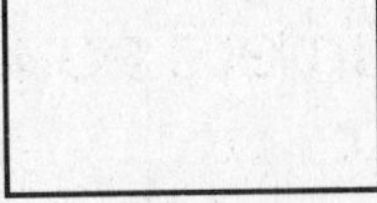

Talia

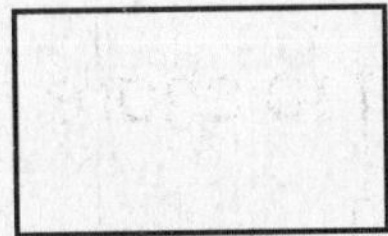

Shane

Natanya

Each child gets _____ counters. $12 \div 4 =$ _____

Name ______________________________

PROBLEM-SOLVING SKILL **R 12-9**

Choose an Operation

Different operations solve different problems. Write the sign that shows the operation you will use to solve the problem; +, −, ×, or ÷.

There are 5 cages at the pet store. 4 puppies are in each cage. How many puppies are at the pet store?

Think about what the problem tells you.

There are __5__ cages. There are __4__ puppies in each cage.

What does the problem want you to find?

How many puppies there are at the pet store.

What operation do you need to use? __×__

Circle the number sentence that solves the problem.

(5 × 4 = 20)   5 + 4 = 9   5 − 4 = 1

So, there are __20__ puppies at the pet store.

Write the sign that shows the operation you need to use.
Circle the number sentence that solves the problem.

1. A cage has 9 birds. Jack buys 3 birds. How many birds are left?

What operation do you need to use? _____

9 + 3 = 12   9 − 3 = 6   9 × 3 = 27

There are _____ birds left at the pet store.

Name ______________________________

PROBLEM-SOLVING APPLICATIONS **R 12-10**

Up, Up, and Away!

Write a number sentence.
Decide what operation you
will use to solve the problem.

5 planes are ready for take-off.
There are 3 pilots on each plane.
How many pilots are on the planes altogether?

What numbers will you use? __5__ and __3__

What operation will you use? Write the sign. __×__

__5__ × __3__ = __15__ __15__ pilots are on the planes.

Solve.

1. There are 73 passengers.
   40 of them order chicken for dinner.
   How many passengers do not order chicken?

   _____ − _____ = _____ passengers

2. A plane has 24 seats in one section.
   There are 3 seats in each row.
   How many rows of seats are there?

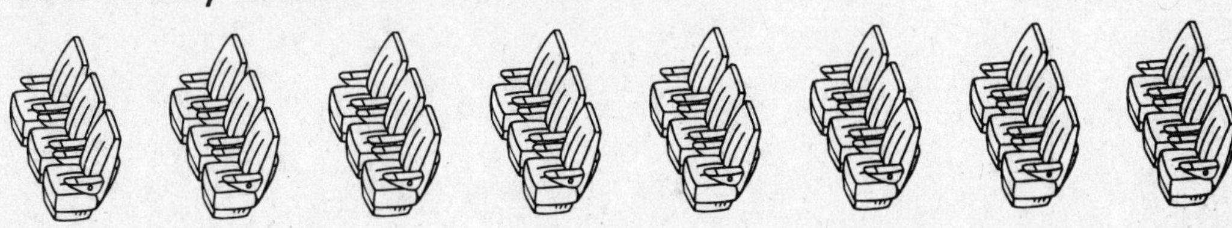

   _____ ÷ _____ = _____ rows of seats